MW00933407

EXCEL 2022

Your Step-By-Step Beginners Guide To Master Excel By Discovering The Best Formulas And Functions, Pivot Tables, Business Modeling, Data Analysis and Macros

JOSEPH THOMPSON

Table of Contents

Introduction 9

Chapter 1: Introduction to Microsoft Excel 11

Understanding Microsoft Excel 11

The history with Advancements in Microsoft Excel 11

Chart of Excel Versions 12

What are some of the Excel Usages? 13

Data Analysis and Interpretation 14

What are the Benefits of Using Microsoft Excel? 15

Formulas 16

Functions 17

The Benefits Of Excel 19

Chapter 2: Getting Started with Excel 23

Download Microsoft Excel 23

Different Ways to Download Excel 23

Excel 2022 Security Improvements 24

Exchange of Dynamic Data (DDE) 25

The Excel Extensions 26

Chapter 3: Exploring the Excel interface 29

What is Excel Interface? 29

Tabs in Excel 30

Ribbon 32

Commands 32

Help 36

Chapter 4: Getting the Best of Excel Formulas 37

Defining an Excel Formula 37

Inserting Formulas in Microsoft Excel 37

To insert the formula by Simple Method 39

To Change a Formula 39

How to Create a Formula by Copying and Pasting in MS Excel 40

Using the Basic Formulas in Excel 42

SUM 42

The Average 43

COUNT 44

IF Statement 45

TRIM 46

MAXIMUM AND MINIMUM 47

Percentage..48

Subtraction...48

Multiplication...49

Division...49

DATE TIME..50

Match..51

How to Use the VLOOKUP Function in MS Excel................52

Financial Formulas..53

How to Use the Random Numbers Generator in Microsoft Excel..............53

Chapter 5: Excel for Beginners 55

Frequently Used Tasks added to Your Toolbar 55

Filter your Data...56

The use of dynamic headers and footers 59

Your print sections 60

Paste Special option 61

Grouping and ungrouping columns to hide extensive data 62

Safety of the spreadsheet and workbook..........................64

Tracing precedents and dependents 65

Data Validation in drop-down menus of a cell 67

Working with Text-to-column..68

How You Can Make the Graph Using Excel........................71

Chapter 6: Excel for Middle-Level Users............................73

The Enhanced Intermediate skills 73

The Pivot Table 74

Conditional Formatting 77

Keyboard Shortcuts to Know...80

Excel Tricks 84

Chapter 7: How Advanced Users can Use Excel.................. 87

Complex Formulas and Functions....................................87

VLOOKUP..87

SUMIF...88

RUNDOWN 89

ROUNDUP..89

TEXT...90

AND...90

COUNT...92

IF combined with AND/OR...92

Functions of CELL, LEFT, MID, and RIGHT 93

PMT and IPMT 93

TRIM.. 94

LEN 94

Upload data from websites... 95

Chapter 8: Tables in Microsoft Excel 97

An overview of Excel tables 97

How to create a table in Microsoft Excel 98

Advantages of using an Excel table 99

Excel table characteristics 100

Chapter 9: Pivot Tables 101

What are Pivot Tables? 101

Why are Pivot Tables Important?...................................... 101

Creating Pivot Tables 102

Sorting Data.. 103

Filtering Data 104

Two-dimensional Pivot Table 106

Chapter 10: Excel Charts... 109

A Basic Understanding of Excel Charts 109

Types of Charts 109

Use of Different Excel Charts 117

Charting Worksheet Data... 117

To Hide or Display Axes 118

To Add Axis Titles... 120

To Move or Remove Chart Title 121

To Add Data Labels 122

To Add a Data Table 122

To Add Error Bars.. 124

To Add Gridlines 125

To Add a Legend 126

To Add a Trendline 128

Adjust a Quick Layout 131

Change the Formatting... 136

Creating Charts in Excel 137

How to Create a Process- Behavior Chart in Excel 140

Chapter 11: Using Excel for Data Analysis........................ 142

Process of carrying out data analysis 142

Why Data Analysis is Important to a Business 144

Major Functions in Data Analysis.................................... 144

Chapter 12: Security in a Spreadsheet and Workbook...................... 151

    How to Lock a Worksheet with Password 151

Chapter 13: Errors in Microsoft Excel 153

    Common Errors in Excel 153

Chapter 14: Macros In MS Excel 155

    How to create a macro in Microsoft Excel 155

    How to run a macro in Excel.. 158

Chapter 15: Excel and Everyday Life 163

Chapter 16: Excel in Business Workspace and Marketplace 167

Conclusion... 171

Introduction

Do you need ways to analyze and make sense of your data? Do you need an easy way to track your budget and expenses, analyze profit, or keep track of your company's inventory? Well, you are in luck. Microsoft Excel 2022 is here to help! Excel is a powerful tool to help you do so, and it's also one of the most popular in the world.

Do you have Microsoft Excel on your PC and laptop? If so, you should have a good idea of how long this version of Excel will last. The software that changed how we work with numbers has largely been replaced by technology and a whole range of other programs, but it just might be coming back in 2022.

Microsoft announced its goal to continue developing Excel in 2022 and beyond as part of its global plan for 2020. They specifically mention their commitment to "real-time coupling analytics with visualizations," which is a key focus for this fall's upgrades.

It's worth noting that Microsoft didn't explicitly refer to Excel 2022. The only mention of 2022 was the company's goal for the coming 12 months: "Our vision for the year 2022 is to couple real-time analytics with visualizations, enabling people to ask and answer questions with data."

This summary of Microsoft's vision in the company's blog post " Microsoft Design + Builds for 2020 " is where they explain that they are planning to provide several new features for Excel. They are hoping to make it "even easier for organizations to access, digest and act on real-time data. Our 2021 roadmap will make this possible through the following capabilities:

Microsoft is not alone in developing these programs; both Google and IBM have similar plans for their competing offerings.

Instead of focusing on specific products, you can consider 2022 as part of a broad trend towards more sophisticated analytics, which will continue to be developed by companies like Google and Microsoft into the foreseeable future.

Undoubtedly, how we use an application like Excel is a strong trend and will only continue in the coming years, but we can be sure that Microsoft will continue to update Excel for much longer than 2022.

This goal does not mean that Microsoft has given up on its plans for new versions of Excel and other programs; it is just a recognition by the company that new technologies are emerging.

Microsoft also makes it clear that it will continue to improve its current products and services, which suggests they do not plan on abandoning products like Word and Excel in favor of newer ones. As they note: "We are also continuing to enhance our existing productivity solutions, such as Office 365, Outlook.com, Excel, PowerPoint, and Word."

It is good to see Microsoft continue to develop its software, even though some of its competitors now have more of an early lead. Knowledge workers can always rely on technology to help them make sense of data and track their finances.

Suppose you're looking for ways to track your budget and expenses or want a simple way of making sense of your profits. In that case, it's worth considering Microsoft's new features for Excel in 2022. You can consider this news as an indication that the software will continue to be developed but without a specific release date.

What are you waiting for? First, start planning for the future

Chapter 1: Introduction to Microsoft Excel

If you're new to Microsoft Excel, you might wonder what you need to know to make the most of the program. In this article, you'll learn what Excel is, how it works, and what types of worksheets you might create. In addition, you'll learn time-saving shortcuts and essential best practices that will make your life easier as you use the software. This Microsoft-approved course will teach you how to get the most out of Microsoft Excel and save you time and money in the long run.

Understanding Microsoft Excel

Excel is a spreadsheet program widely used in business and other fields. Its versatile features make it a valuable tool for a variety of tasks. Most office professionals today use Excel to manage data, make reports, and analyze numbers. Even the most mundane workbooks can become more appealing with the help of MS Excel's charts. Its pivot table feature helps create complex reports, charts, and calculations.

In addition to its calculation and graphing capabilities, Excel also features a macro programming language called VBA. VBA is included in Excel and can be used to create custom functions in the spreadsheet. For example, the following subroutine will calculate the square of a column variable named x and then write the result into the cell y. It will then do the same function on the other cells in the workbook but with an additional cell named y.

If you want to create a spreadsheet on a computer, you should have access to MS Excel. MS Excel can be used by businesses and individuals and is widely used in educational institutions and business settings. Spreadsheets are grids of data with columns, rows, and cells. These cells are also known as 'cells,' which is the cells' name. The cells are located on the left-hand side of the worksheet.

The original version of Microsoft Excel came out in 1985 when Lotus Development Corporation sold it to Microsoft. The Lotus 1-2-3 spreadsheet application, which ran on MS-DOS, was sold to a different company. Demand for this spreadsheet program skyrocketed in the 1980s, so Microsoft purchased the company and merged it with Lotus. The program was a success and quickly became one of the most popular business applications. With countless features, Excel continues to grow.

The history of Advancements in Microsoft Excel

The brief history of Microsoft Excel begins with the first spreadsheet application. Known as MultiPlan, it was developed for the MS-DOS and CP/M systems. The program was later renamed Excel and was beaten by Lotus 1-2-3 on MS-DOS platforms. Excel's graphical interface was introduced in 1985, but it was only available on Apple Macs. As Microsoft began to develop its Windows operating system, it re-engineered Excel for Windows and released version 2.0 in 1987.

While Excel is used for many purposes today, its origins are very interesting. This application is widely used by millions of people, making it a basic tool in many different fields. This powerful software has made intensive numerical analysis accessible to the masses. Its features, such as functions, have allowed it to become an indispensable tool for managing finances and working processes. With its various automation capabilities, Excel makes calculating large data sets simple. There are many ways to use an Excel spreadsheet.

An attorney and privacy activist developed Microsoft Excel as the first electronic spreadsheet. Its development dated back to 1978 and was developed to compete with VisiCalc. The spreadsheet application's popularity led to Microsoft's eventual IPO in 1986. Microsoft's spreadsheet program has become the industry's most popular business application. This is partly due to its gentle learning curve and almost complete interoperability.

Today, more businesses are moving toward cloud-based computing, which provides multi-user data analytics and analysis access. With this expansion, Microsoft will continue to develop and enhance Excel to meet user needs. However, the future of data analysis is highly dependent on its flexibility. In the meantime, the future of Excel is bright. With so many applications available in the cloud, it's essential to know how to leverage them to make better business decisions.

The Microsoft Office applications communicate with each other and can use the capabilities of other programs. This feature is called Dynamic Data Exchange and is widely used in the financial markets. It enables applications to access essential financial data services. As with other spreadsheets, Excel can work with external data sources through ODBC. One such application is Power Plus Pro. For more information on Excel, check out the company's website.

Chart of Excel Versions

#	Name	Released
1	Version 1	1985
2	Excel 2	1987
3	Excel 3	1990
4	Excel 4	1992
5	Excel 5	1993
6	Excel 95	1995
7	Excel 97	1997
8	Excel 2000	1999
9	Excel 2002	2001
10	Microsoft Office Excel 2003	2003

11	Microsoft Office Excel 2007	2007
12	Microsoft Office Excel 2010	2010
13	Microsoft Excel 2013	2013
14	Microsoft Excel 2016	2016
15	Microsoft Excel 2019	2019
16.	Microsoft Excel 2021	2021

What are some of the Excel Usages?

You've probably heard of examples of Excel usage, including preparing and presenting budgets for team outings, calculating employee discounts based on monthly purchase volume, and generating revenue growth models for new products. But did you know that Excel has many uses than just spreadsheets and financial reports? These examples are only a handful of ways to use this powerful software. Keep reading to learn more. The possibilities are almost limitless.

Functions are predefined formulas that perform calculations using specific values in a given order. Most spreadsheet programs have a variety of common functions to help you find ranges of cells quickly. Learn about each function's syntax and different parts, including arguments and cell references. To use a function effectively, you'll want to know how it works in practice. Here are three examples of Excel usage:

Many businesses use Excel extensively for day-to-day operations. These operations can involve complicated logistics, and it's essential to keep track of inventory flows to avoid overstocking and ensure the smooth running of daily operations. In addition, excel's powerful functions make it a valuable tool for managing daily office activities. For example, an Excel spreadsheet can store records for individual employees, including name, email address, start date, purchase history, subscription status, and last contact.

Databases divide data into columns, and the DATEDIF function uses two fields to determine a person's age. To use this function, you'll need their date of birth and their current date. Another useful Excel function is VLOOKUP, which looks up a value in the leftmost column of a table and returns its value. If you're using Excel, you can do the same thing in a database, albeit more sophisticated.

If you're using Excel for the first time, you may want to explore the various functions it offers. For example, the VLOOKUP function performs a vertical lookup in the leftmost column. When it returns a value from a particular column, it uses the same cell as the previous one. By learning how to use these functions, you'll be able to manipulate data much more efficiently than a formula. So, take a few minutes to familiarize yourself with the basics of Excel usage.

Whether you're new to Excel or are already an experienced user, these examples of how to use this software will help you get started on the right foot. These examples cover data analysis and interpretation, goal setting and organization, and more.

In Education Field

Teachers should give students plenty of opportunities to explore Excel's many features and capabilities. Table layouts, forms, infographics, data tools, and algorithms are some tools that teachers might use to train students in the classroom. Using it in class allows students to see how theory is applied in practical situations and will enable them to explore large amounts of data quickly and easily. The benefits of using Excel in education go far beyond learning to do complex calculations. Students may also learn to use logical formulas, such as SUMIF or IF, to analyze data.

For example, using the calendar function in Excel to analyze data is a great way to keep track of different commitments. Students can use it to keep track of their classes and their schedules. They can also create event columns and filter them using the COUNTIF() function. In addition, they can use SUMIF() to add values to a column if they match the criteria. Students will find the calendar feature invaluable in the field of education.

Despite being a common software, many students have limited experience and may not be familiar with the program. Teachers should try integrating Excel into their K-12 curriculums across various subject areas. In the third grade, students should be introduced to the basics of Excel. Excel can be confusing, and students may be tempted to check the work before handing it to their peers. For this reason, teachers should introduce students to Excel early in their educational careers.

The Commercial Sector

Many businesses use Excel to manage day-to-day activities. Many of these activities require intricate logistics, and inventory flows must be controlled to avoid overstocking. Excel is also used to keep track of supplier and client transactions, critical dates, and time schedules. It is an all-purpose tool for office managers. In addition to accounting, Microsoft Excel is also used in strategic analysis and financial management. Excel can guide business decisions by keeping track of these metrics, such as how much to spend on certain assets.

The Commercial Sector in Microsoft Excel is an essential program for day-to-day operations. Many businesses use this application to analyze data, perform calculations, and organize client sales lists. Moreover, the data visualization capabilities of this software allow businesses to make smart decisions based on the results. Using pivot tables and smart arts, Microsoft Excel can help you stay on top of business trends. In addition, it can automate many business tasks and save time creating data.

In summary, Excel is a versatile tool for commercial purposes. Microsoft Excel is the way to go if you are looking for a solution for your business.

Data Analysis and Interpretation

Excel is a useful tool for data analysis and interpretation. It includes built-in pivot tables, which can significantly help when analyzing large datasets. Data analysis requires sorting data. Once you have sorted your data, you can use other tools to make the data easier to read and understand.

Descriptive statistics are the most basic statistical tools that Excel offers. They help you summarize a dataset and provide information about its central tendency, variability, outlier detection, etc. Excel is a good choice for basic data management and statistical analysis. Excel is a useful tool if you are working on a data-rich project and need to show your results to the C-Suite. You can use the Data Visualization tool to create a graph to display your findings.

Understanding the terms covariance, correlation, and regression for advanced Excel users can help create better data visualizations. Correlation, for example, allows you to identify the patterns between two variables. Covariance, on the other hand, identifies variables that change together. Regression, on the other hand, determines how often one variable changes. In addition, excel allows for single and multiple regressions.

Goals Organizing and Preparing

If you are unsure how to manage your goals, creating a spreadsheet is an excellent way to get started. With the help of Microsoft Excel, it is possible to set financial, professional, and physical goals. In addition to that, they can help you accomplish your goals faster.

Advanced Excel training will help you become a powerful employee by helping you manage your work more efficiently. As a result, more productive employees can complete tasks faster and provide better customer service. Furthermore, advanced Excel users can create tracking systems for various operations, departments, and workflow processes. These benefits are invaluable for any employee and will allow you to move on to higher-level positions.

Microsoft Excel is a powerful tool for project management. You can create simple to-do lists, checklists, and more. It also can create waterfall charts and kanban-style boards. You can also manage projects using various charts in Excel. The best part about using Excel for project management is that it allows you to easily create and modify charts of all types. If you're looking for a simple way to manage your project, you can use Excel for task management.

What are the Benefits of Using Microsoft Excel?

MS Excel comes with analytical tools to make large-scale data analysis a snap. Its features include filtering, sorting, and searching capabilities and the ability to create charts, pivot tables, and graphs. These features enhance the ability to organize and classify information. These benefits make MS Excel a valuable tool for various applications, from personal finance to business analysis. For more information, check out the benefits of using MS Excel to make a business decision.

MS Excel comes with numerous options for formatting, including bold and italics. These options can highlight important data or accounting information. In addition, you can select a suitable color scheme by clicking the Quick Analysis button or the Formatting tab. This feature allows you to format data in a way that makes it easy to read and understand. The tool also includes a range of formatting options. Its advanced formatting options can help you create a more appealing presentation.

Advanced users of Excel can develop complex spreadsheets for managing and tracking information about people. They can maintain complex financial and inventory accounts. They can create tracking systems for departments, operations, and workflow processes. This allows them to progress to higher positions due to their expertise. Your business can benefit from all the tools and benefits of using Microsoft Excel. If you're wondering what the benefits of using MS Excel are, consider the following:

Accessibility: Microsoft Excel is widely compatible with third-party applications. Its cloud computing features allow it to access Excel documents from multiple devices. This makes it an ideal tool for remote working. Furthermore, the Vlookup feature allows combining data from multiple sources into a document. In addition to its robust database, Excel is compatible with various devices, including smartphones. This means you don't have to sit in front of a computer all day to work on a file.

Besides being versatile, Excel helps you manage your time better. Excel has many shortcuts and functions that make navigating and performing various tasks easier. For example, you can export data from an Excel sheet to other programs, like Outlook or Word. Then, you can use that data in various programs and save time. As a result, you'll be more productive and happier at your job by automating mundane tasks. You'll also enjoy more efficient workflows and happier employees.

Formulas

You can write complex formulas if you are looking for more advanced features in Microsoft Excel. Excel provides many functions to choose from. If you do not know what type of formula you want to use, you can type it in the Insert Function dialogue box and click the Enter key. Once you have entered a formula, you can type a description in the cell below it or browse the list. You can then select the function that you want to use.

The simplest formulas in Excel are math equations. These use standard operators, including the plus sign (+), minus sign (-), backslash (/), and an asterisk (*). The part of the equation that should be calculated first is enclosed in parentheses. Using multiple sets of parentheses is possible for complex math equations. You can protect the worksheet by using a password to add extra protection.

Functions are more efficient than formulas. For example, you can use the SUM function to calculate the average value of a range of cells. You can also use the COUNTBLANK function to count the number of empty cells in a range. These functions are similar to formulas in Microsoft Excel but can be more complex. These functions can be tricky to remember, but they're essential for any advanced user. When you're learning to use formulas in Microsoft Excel, you should start by practicing them with simple tasks. For example, you can add two numbers to cells A1 and A2.

In addition to using functions, you can also create your formulas in Excel. These can perform complex calculations and manipulate data. For example, you can use the sum function, the average function, the blank count function, the Vlookup function, and Xlookup. You can also use the if function, and it can be used in complex calculations. Arithmetic functions and other mathematical operations can be done using Excel's single formula

Functions

There are many functions available in Microsoft Excel that help you perform mathematical operations. For example, the "IS" function returns sensitive information to the current folder or directory. You can also use the "me avail" function to determine the total number of bytes of available memory. Similarly, "num file" displays the total number of active worksheets in a workbook. There are nine functions in Excel:

If you're trying to perform a complicated calculation, you'll need to use the advanced functions of Microsoft Excel. These functions will help you perform complex calculations or data analysis. The goal seeks function to enable you to change your assumptions and make new ones, which is helpful in a trial-and-error approach. For example, you can search for "sum" and enter "2" as input. Then, when you're finished, you can use "sudden" to find the sum of two numbers.

The SUM function aggregates values in a range, row by row. In this case, you'd type A2 to A7, B4 to B17, and so on. You'd then use the SUM function to sum the values in those cells. The COUNT function is similar to the SUM function but returns the number of cells based on its ranking in ascending or descending order. Finally, RANK returns the rank of a number within a range.

Using its functions, you can perform all sorts of operations on data in MS Excel. They include averaging a range of cells, modifying text, and adding data to a cell range. You can also do simple calculations, such as adding the total of two cells. However, you'll have to seek advanced training to learn more advanced Excel functions. Once you're familiar with the basics, you can begin using your new spreadsheet.

Auto-fill

The Auto-fill feature in Microsoft Excel allows you to automatically enter a series of data based on the values entered in a range of cells. For example, this feature can also be used to enter a row of months. The Auto-fill feature in Excel can be turned on or off to customize the fill method. By default, Excel enters a series of values in every cell that contains the first value of a column or row.

Double-click the fill handle in the lower-right corner of the active cell to turn Auto-fill on or off. You can also double-click the fill handle to only fill a selected cell's formatting. Alternatively, you can click the Auto-fill handle to fill the cell manually. Either way, you can customize the Auto-fill handle by choosing the desired option from the drop-down list. The Auto-fill feature is especially useful when repeating a series of values.

To turn on and off the Auto-fill feature, first select a cell. You will see selection handles in the upper-left and lower-right corners. Then, tap the Touch tool to summon a mini-toolbar, a row of command buttons that terminates with a Show Context Menu button. Once you've tapped the Show Context Menu button, Excel will add the Auto-fill button to the currently selected cell. The Auto-fill button appears as a blue downward-pointing arrow in the lower-right corner of a cell. Drag the Auto-fill button through a column or row of cells until you find the right value.

There are other ways to use the Auto-fill feature in Microsoft Excel. The Fill Year option searches for patterns in the year when filling a cell. For example, Fill Year will use a pattern in the year to fill a cell with the correct value. This option is excellent for filling dates in MS Excel. It's especially useful if you're unsure of the format of a number. The Fill Series and Fill Days options work well for dates.

Color-theme

In Microsoft Excel, you can customize the look of your workbook by using color schemes. Colour schemes are sets of eight coordinating colors for text, objects, and formatting. When you select one, you'll see a small preview of the colors you can change. Changes will be applied to your document's text, shapes, SmartArt graphics, and other elements. You can change the colors for any of these areas to make your spreadsheet look more professional.

You can create color sheets in Excel 2010 by holding the CTRL key as you click the sheet tabs. For example, in the Format menu, click Sheet and then Tab Color. Then, click the color you want to use, and then click OK. Using more than one color sheet, you can create a macro to sort your sheets by color. You can also use a small letter prefix to make your sheets more organized.

Change your theme colors in Word or Excel. Choose the color scheme that best represents your business. You can change the font and size of the text, as well as the color of the background and text. Using different theme colors, you can change your document's background color, fonts, and other formatting elements. If you're having trouble changing the color of a cell in Excel, see the video below. Once you've created a custom color scheme, you can then apply it to all your workbooks.

Customizing your workbook can be done easily by using a theme. Excel has themes built-in to give you more control over your design. There are also custom themes available for Excel, which allow you to make changes to fonts, colors, effects, and more. For example, you can customize the colors, fonts, and font effects when working on a project to make them more appealing. Once you've selected a color theme, you can change the settings of the colors and fonts to create a unique style for your workbook.

Data recovery

Having lost a workbook in Microsoft Excel? Then, there are several options to recover it. Unfortunately, deleted files are often not retrievable unless the user has backed up the file. However, suppose you have turned on backups. In that case, you can recover lost data in Excel by restoring earlier versions of a file. Locate the file you wish to restore and click the "Down" arrow to bring up the options menu.

If you cannot find a backup file of your file in Excel, try using OneDrive to recover it. If the file is on OneDrive, you can right-click the file and choose "View version history." This process is especially useful when the file has been accidentally deleted and may have been corrupted or altered. It can also recover deleted files that contain essential information. Finally, you can use OneDrive to recover lost files if you accidentally formatted a disk and no longer have access to it.

Another way to recover data from Excel is to try to save it again. For example, if your workbook has crashed, it is possible to recover unsaved files using Excel's recovery options. This way, you can restore the file with the previous version by saving it again. This process can be performed several times to restore lost data. You can also use the 'Restore Previous Version' option to restore the file to its original state.

Before you begin the data recovery process, make sure you create a directory where you will store the recovered files. First, select the data you need to recover. If the data is corrupted, select 'Repair' or 'Extract Data' to recover the data. However, this option will not fix the corrupt workbook but will try to recover most of the data in the workbook. If you cannot recover data with this option, you can try to use a third-party tool.

The Benefits Of Excel

When appropriately used, Microsoft Excel can boost your job performance and productivity. It can help you analyze and organize information with ease. This section will highlight some of the benefits of using this program. After reading it, you'll be well on becoming more productive and gaining technical skills.

Improving job performance

Learning Excel is a highly beneficial skill for any company. It makes repetitive tasks easier to complete, allowing you to focus more on other things instead of worrying about how to calculate a simple calculation. Additionally, knowing how to use Excel will save you time and effort. You can save countless hours by learning how to use Excel and using it to your advantage. The numerous benefits of knowing how to use Excel for your job performance.

One of the many uses for Microsoft Excel is as a contract administrator. It is an efficient way to track details about contracts. You can find template contracts and adjust them based on contract lifecycle stages and types. Account managers, for example, are expected to use Excel in their work. They handle customer records and generally need to know how to use them to track their sales and expenses. You can also use it to manage your inventory.

Improves technical skills

Using advanced Excel techniques can help your employees perform business tasks more efficiently. For example, advanced users can maintain complex financial and inventory accounts and create tracking systems for different operations and workflow processes. As a result, they can improve productivity, increase efficiency, and deliver better customer service. Further, these skills can lead to advancement in your company and a higher salary. Are you interested in acquiring advanced Excel skills? Continue reading for tips and tricks to make the most of this powerful program.

Advanced Microsoft Excel skills are extremely desirable. Advanced Excel skills will make your life easier and your work more efficient. In addition, you'll stand out among other employees and boost your employee morale! In addition to increasing your salary, learning to use advanced Excel tools will improve your work-life balance.

Improved productivity

Learn how to customize Microsoft Excel to fit your preferences and boost your productivity. This free spreadsheet program provides several customization options to improve productivity and boost your staff's confidence. For example, if you want your numbers to round to the hundredths or change the default file location, Excel can do the job. In addition, you can customize it to your liking by following a few basic steps.

Advanced Excel tools increase your speed and accuracy. Excel users can quickly analyze and complete tasks with advanced tools and functions. Advanced tools in Excel enable you to keep team members informed, organize your work, and streamline workflow processes. Advanced tools can save you valuable time and effort. Following these tips can make your workday more productive and save money.

Can easily examine and organize information

Advanced users of Microsoft Excel can solve many business problems and develop tracking systems for operations and workflow processes. They can maintain intricate inventory and financial accounts and create complex workflow processes with advanced skills. Advanced users can even advance to higher positions, such as financial analysts. For example, you can use Excel to sort and organize employee profiles and expenses if you work in human resources. In addition, you can create pivot tables to analyze data and summarize information from worksheets.

Many essential features of Excel are found under the Data menu, including imports, connections to databases, removing duplicates, and data validation. You can use data validation to ensure consistency between cells. The Review menu contains many collaborative tasks, such as making comments in cells and restricting permissions. With this menu, you can easily analyze data and determine where changes need to be made. This menu is also helpful for working with other people.

A balanced monitoring system

If you are a manager, you may be interested in learning how to create a balanced scorecard and operational dashboards using Microsoft Excel. Both tools are used to measure organizational performance and are in high demand in large organizations. A balanced monitoring system with Excel combines the benefits of performance management with the power of data visualization.

Solve complex problems

If you're unsure how to use Microsoft Excel, you've come to the right place. You can use Excel to solve complicated problems with ease. Spreadsheets are an excellent way to break complex problems into simple steps. Each step requires the input of one cell, an action to be performed on that value, and the results output into another cell. In addition, you can use spreadsheets to output results to the outer limits of a worksheet if necessary.

You'll need to load the Solver add-in when you first open Excel. Then, activate the Solver command in the Tools menu. Once you have Solver loaded, you're ready to solve a problem. The Solver add-in has many examples of problems you can solve. In addition, you can select as many constraints as you need for your specific problem. This add-in will allow you to solve a variety of optimization problems.

Saves time

If you are using Microsoft Excel for work, you are probably aware of its many features and tools. By using these shortcuts and tools, you can improve the integrity of your workbooks and save time. In addition, with the proper organization of your files, you can analyze and make decisions more easily.

Using keyboard shortcuts and Quick Access Toolbars can be helpful if you need to repeat a process often. Using the F4 key can also help you automate repetitive tasks. Pressing this key repeatedly will repeat the action you last performed.

Manages your budgets

If you are a novice at managing budgets, consider learning to use Microsoft Excel. With the help of a template, you can easily track your monthly budget. This tool calculates the difference between income and expenses and the projected and actual costs of monthly expenses. Examples of monthly expenses include utility bills, credit card bills, gym memberships, and movie subscriptions. Managing your budget with Excel will save you time, money, and headaches in the future.

Another great feature of Excel is its ability to sort data. For example, if you're planning a vacation, you can sort the spreadsheet to show you which hotel room has the best price. Similarly, you can sort by price if you compare airline ticket costs. This will reveal the best deals and save time typing the same variable in every cell. Another feature of Excel is its ability to convert data from one column to another.

Chapter 2: Getting Started with Excel

If you are new to Microsoft Excel, you may wonder how to start. This article will show you how to download Microsoft Excel, different ways to download Excel, and why you should buy it. It also covers how to use Excel and its various Extensions. You'll also learn how to import and export data. Using Excel is easy once you know the basics. After all, it's one of the most popular spreadsheet applications on the market today.

Download Microsoft Excel

If you've ever needed to organize or manipulate large amounts of data, you've probably considered downloading Microsoft Excel. The program is one of the most popular ways to organize data, create graphs for presentations, or solve complex equations. Unfortunately, there's a steep learning curve. The more advanced functions in Excel require a deeper understanding of the software. However, if you're a beginner, you can still get the most out of the software by manually entering data or learning basic formulas.

The first step in learning to use Excel is downloading and installing the software on your computer. It's a great idea to start small and practice using the program before moving on to more advanced features. The program includes many useful tools, including auto-fill features. For example, learn to make your column titles visible and to sort data alphabetically. You should also start with simple data, such as your company's sales figures, and then expand on that knowledge over time.

Spreadsheets can make your life much easier. Excel's powerful computational abilities make it a favorite for accountants and other professionals who need to organize data. Marketers can use the program to track information and use charts to improve their campaigns. It also has a variety of shortcuts and quick fixes, making it an excellent tool for tracking data and developing marketing campaigns. You'll be amazed by its capabilities and ease of use!

The best part about using Excel is that you can do everything in the program. If you want to collaborate with others, you'll be able to share your spreadsheets with them offline, either by copying them from your OneDrive folder or accessing them through Excel Online. In addition, once you have synchronized your files with Excel Online, you can view and edit them online. These advantages make it an essential tool for any businessperson.

Different Ways to Download Excel

If you are looking for different ways to download Microsoft Excel, you may wonder which method is the best. In the past, there were a few ways you could download Microsoft Excel. It was possible to download an older program version from the Microsoft website. However, Microsoft has largely discontinued older versions of Excel and is pushing people to upgrade. However, if you are interested in downloading an older version of Excel, you may still find it online. You can download it with the help of a product key, but this option is risky.

Another way to download Microsoft Excel is to purchase a software version. It can be expensive if you try to buy it by itself, but you can always buy a suite of other Microsoft Office software to avoid the price tag. However, if you don't want to spend that much, you can download it for free and save it to your hard drive. Alternatively, you can get it through a subscription to Microsoft 365, which includes the Mac version of Excel.

One of the best ways to download Microsoft Excel is through a subscription to Microsoft's 365 suite. Unfortunately, this means that you need to pay for the software after the first month. The browser-based version of Excel is fine if you're looking for essential functions and formulas, but it doesn't have additional features and security. Besides, you might encounter viruses and other malware if you download them illegally.

Another way to download Microsoft Excel is to use the free web version. The web version is stripped down, so you can compare it to Google Sheets. Both of these services should offer the basic functions of Excel. Alternatively, you can also download Microsoft Office mobile applications. These are available for most modern devices and work on Android and iOS. The Microsoft Excel app also features OneDrive integration, which is another plus. You can use any of these methods to download Microsoft Excel.

For older Chromebooks, you can use the Chrome Web Store. Navigate to the Extensions tab and search for Office Online or Microsoft Excel. Microsoft Excel Online is similar to the desktop version, but you can use it in any browser. You must also have a Microsoft Account to use Excel Online. Then, the file you've saved will be saved in your OneDrive account. This way, you can save and access your file from anywhere.

You can download the alternative version of Microsoft Excel from the official Microsoft website. You may either buy it or try it for free. On the website, fill out the registration form. This software is offered in a variety of plans and licenses. There are two types of licenses: home and business. Take a look at the plans and prices for these licenses. There are three sorts of licenses for the Home license. One is for personal use, the second is for a household of 2 to 6 people, and the third is for a student who can only use one computer or laptop. For a year, the prices are different for each one. Four Business One plans are Basic, Standard, Premium, and Apps for Business. Each plan has its own set of features and annual costs.

Companies combine them to gain various features and better functionality based on their needs.

Excel 2022 Security Improvements

With the January 2022 update, Microsoft has made some security improvements to Excel. These include disabling Dynamic Data Exchange (DDE) and automatically activating OLE objects. This change affects all supported versions of Excel, including Office 365. However, users should note that the January 2022 update does not affect users who previously configured DDE settings. Instead, Office users can disable this feature by editing the appropriate registry value. Administrators can then enable DDE server launch through Group Policy.

The Office 365 security update can be installed relatively soon as long as no problems are reported. The update also fixes several bugs, including an error when rendering code in Outlook. If you're concerned about the security of your Office 365 subscription, the Microsoft Excel 2022 security improvements are essential.

Another security feature introduced with the Office 365 build is a feature that lets users unhide multiple sheets at once. In addition to this feature, Outlook has an updated Contacts view list. The Teams feature allows users to add a channel to the calendar tab and send reactions during meetings. Finally, users must apply sensitivity labels on all Office applications to prevent the risk of exploits. This feature is available in the Office 365 beta program.

Exchange of Dynamic Data (DDE)

There are a few essential rules to follow when using the Microsoft Excel Exchange of Dynamic Data feature. The data ranges must be contiguous, meaning that the data should not be entered in different rows or columns. Dynamic ranges must also be named appropriately and updated regularly to avoid errors. The series names must be named appropriately, too. You cannot use the same labels for column and row headings and dynamic range names.

The first thing to fix this problem is to ensure the DDE settings are correct. This will prevent Excel from opening individual files. If this setting is set to 'Ignore other applications that use DDE,' you cannot open Excel. The same applies to the Export in Query Ready Mode option in the browser and exporting balances from Financial Reporting. Click the Microsoft Office button, and then select Options. In the Advanced category, click General. Click the check box next to the 'Ignore other applications that use DDE.' Then, restart Excel.

DDE is a standard Windows program that provides information to other applications. For example, a custom in-house application might use DDE to open a Microsoft Excel spreadsheet. This application would then send commands to the Microsoft Excel spreadsheet. However, DDE has been replaced by the Component Object Model (COM) since Windows 95. Excel's extensive OLE Automation object model is now the recommended method for communicating with Excel. However, DDE is still used when financial data is exchanged.

Controls to stop DDE server lookup and DDE server launch were introduced to all supported Excel versions in January 2018.

DDE server launch was disabled in Office 365 versions >= 1902 in August 2019, and Group Policy support for both DDE server lookup and DDE server launch was enabled.

DDE server launch is disabled in Office 2021, although Group Policy support for both DDE configurations is available.

In Office 2016 and Office 2019, the January 2022 update disables the server of DDE to launch in all supported versions of Excel and adds Group Policy support for this option. This update will not impact users who have already specified these settings.

Importance of Buying Excel

If you're looking to save money on software for your computer, you might wonder, "Why should I buy Microsoft Excel?" It has been one of the most popular programs in the world, and it can be a valuable tool if you're looking to do some serious spreadsheet work. Microsoft Excel is a spreadsheet program that stores data in a specific format (a column and row intersection are called a cell). These files are known as workbooks and can be incredibly useful if you want to analyze and present the data clearly and concisely.

Microsoft Excel can be downloaded online if you're looking for a cheap way to create presentations. You can also get it as part of the Office 365 package, which includes Microsoft Word, PowerPoint, OneDrive, Teams, and Skype. All you need to access Office 365 is a Microsoft Account, which you can create for free. You can use Excel Online, but the free version has limited features. You can unlock more features if you sign up for the Excel Online Premium Plan.

When you purchase the Excel 2022:

- You have perpetual permission meaning you can use the software indefinitely
- There are low risks of being hacked
- You get more improved features, especially for funnel charts and pivot tables
- The latest version has more consistency

The Excel Extensions

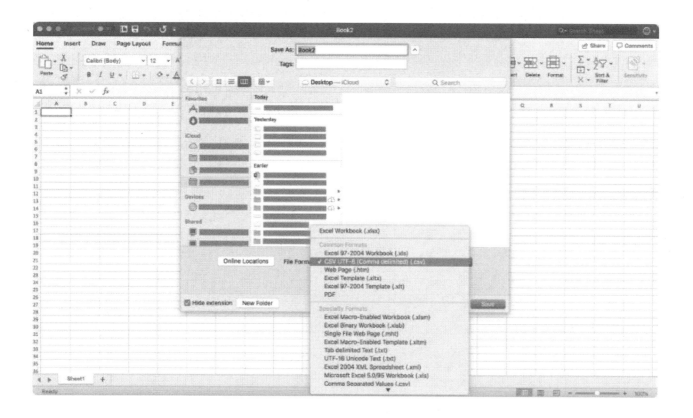

You've probably noticed that Excel files come with various file extensions. You can check which type of yours is by looking at the Excel file Type dropdown menu. The extension also describes the file type, so you can decide whether you want to use that file type. Here are some ways to tell which file extension you're working with.

This tutorial is for the most recent versions of Excel. However, previous versions of Excel might be slightly different. You can also download a blank workbook to reference while following along. But the best part about this tutorial is that it works with all recent versions of Excel.

Excel is one tool that allows us to save files in several formats. The.xlsx extension is a standard Excel extension for storing basic types of data. Another default extension that was used till MS Office 2007 is XLS. We have XLSM for storing VBA code. It is designed explicitly for macros. CSV (Comma Separated Values) is another extension that delimits data separated by commas. The XLSB extension is used for compressing, storing, and opening files, among other things.

In addition to the Ribbon, you can use other Excel features, such as dialogue boxes. These are float-over windows that float above the active Excel application window. The dialogue boxes can display information, sign-in pages, request confirmation, and even host videos. You can also access the Dialog API for Office Add-ins. Using the Dialog API, you can create an Excel add-in that interacts with the content of your workbook.

Suppose you want to write code in Excel. In that case, you can use Visual Basic for Applications (VBA), a dialect of Visual Basic. This language provides programming capabilities that make spreadsheets more versatile. Aside from that, it also offers compatibility with earlier versions. In addition, many more Excel extensions are available, so you can explore them and see which ones will work best for you.

Once you have a basic idea of the types of files that you can open in Excel, you can move on to using the VBA programming language. You can even use VBA to create VBA macros in Excel. VBA provides a comprehensive API that makes it easy to write custom Excel macros. So, what are you waiting for? Get started today!

Here are some of the common file extensions:

The Excel file extension is XLS.

It is the most popular and default extension form in Microsoft Office spreadsheets. XLS was the file extension before Excel 2007. This extension refers to a file that includes various data, formats, and images, among other things. With the aid of an extension, the operating system detects the file type and opens it in the Excel program. From Excel 2.0 through Excel 2003, the XLS file format is the default.

The Excel file extension is XLSX.

This extension is used by spreadsheet files created with Excel 2007 and later versions. The current default file extension for an Excel file is XLSX.

The XSLX file format is based on XML. Using this technique, the XSLX file format is much lighter and smaller than the XLS file format, resulting in significant space savings compared to the XLS file format. Downloading and uploading excel documents takes less time. The only downside of this XSLX extension is that it is incompatible with files created before Excel 2007.

Excel file extension XLSM

This file extension is created by spreadsheets starting with Excel 2007 and containing Excel macros.

It's simple to recognize that a file includes a macro with the help of an extension. This version exists for security reasons and safeguards a file from computer viruses, harmful macros, infecting machines, and other threats. In terms of macros and security, this file extension is extremely dependable.

Excel file extension XLSB

This file extension type completely allows the compressing, storing, and opening of excel files that contain a vast quantity of data or information.

The opening and processing of an excel file containing a huge quantity of data take a long time. It hangs up sometimes when opening and regularly crashes.

Chapter 3: Exploring the Excel interface

There are several ways to explore the Microsoft Excel interface. First, learn how to use the various tabs to access important information. Excel comes with more than a dozen different cursor shapes. You'll learn which ones do what when you explore these shapes. You can also use the mouse to select any cell in the worksheet. Clicking on a cell will make it active. A name box will appear for the active cell. Once you've changed the cell, you can save or change your work.

What is Excel Interface?

The interface is composed of several components that make up Excel. These components are the Workbook Components and the Ribbon. The Ribbon contains commands, groups, and buttons. Each tab has a different function and is categorized based on its usage. For example, the Home tab contains buttons for the most frequently used functions. The Ribbon also has tabs for Inserting, Formatting, Data, Review, and Clipboard. The Ribbon can be used to move between different sections of the workbook or between individual workbooks.

The user interface in Microsoft Excel has a few key elements. The status bar displays some common information, and the zoom slider controls the size of the worksheet. It can also be customized. Here are some of the other components of the Excel interface. The ribbon contains tabs and other icons that control the application's functions. Once you've chosen a tab, go to its properties and choose a color scheme. You can also adjust the background of the workspace and change the background color.

The title bar of the spreadsheet shows the name of the active document. The upper-right corner has control buttons that allow you to change the sheet label, share it, and close the workbook. Other interface elements in Excel include the diskette and excel icon. In addition, the menu bar has commands like File, Insert, Page Layout, Formulas, Data, Review, and the Help tab with a light bulb icon. All menus have subcategories to simplify the distribution of information and calculation.

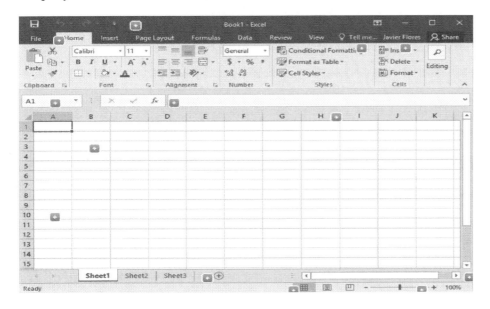

Tabs in Excel

File

There are various ways to organize the information you store on your file tabs in Microsoft Excel. For example, the Office Tab consolidates actions such as saving and closing multiple files. This tab is also used to organize the files in your Favorites Group. You can also customize the size of the tabs. You can set the length of the tabs to be automatic, self-adaptive, or fixed. The auto-adaptive option displays most file names, and the fixed option shows the same length for all tabs.

All your Excel worksheet operational aspects are here in the File Tab. The INFO section gives you a chance to set a given password to your workbook to ensure no one else can modify it when you are not around.

Use the NEW option under File to come up with a new worksheet. In addition, you may use the keyboard shortcut Ctrl+N or Command+N (for Mac users).

The OPEN option allows you to open and work on a previously saved file. Choosing the option will open a directory where you are supposed to choose your file's location.

The SAVE option ensures that everything you are working on is stored and up to date every time you select the option.

Other options include share, print, close, and export.

Quick Access Toolbar

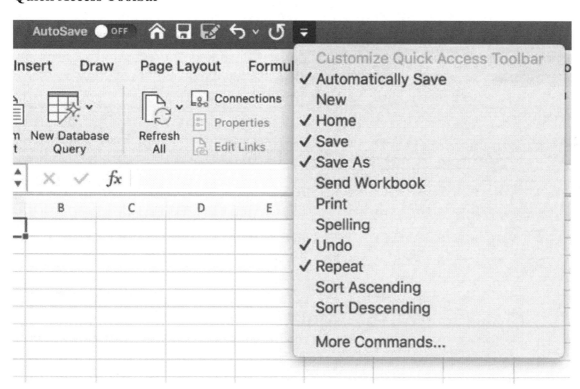

The Quick Access Toolbar is located in the upper left corner of the Excel program. Save, Undo, and Redo are part of the Quick Access Toolbar's default commands. Clicking the little downward arrow at the right end of the toolbar brings up a customization dialogue box where you may add or remove icons from the toolbar.

Tell me

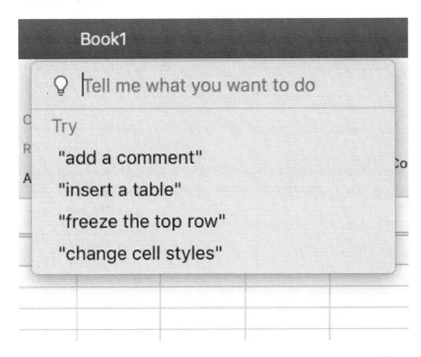

The tell me search box in the user interface allows for quick and easy locating commands without going to a ribbon tab or group. Instead, type here any command you wish to use.

Title Bar

The name presently in use is shown in the title bar at the top of the excel spreadsheet program. The bar places the workbook's name at the center.

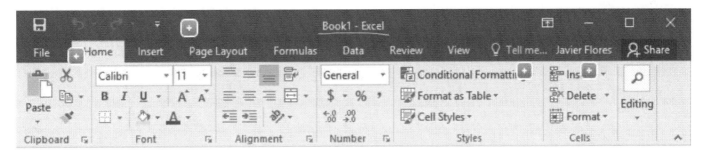

Book1- Excel is the name of the workbook.

Ribbon

The ribbon is the primary working element of the Microsoft Excel interface and includes all instructions necessary to do most basic operations. You will realize it is divided into tabs with a set or group of commands.

Excel Ribbon Tabs

The Excel ribbon has nine tabs: File, Home, Insert, Page Layout, Formulas, Data, Review, View, and Help. You can add additional tabs with your preferred command buttons, like Draw and Developer, to create a customized Ribbon.

Home

Contains the most often used commands, such as copy and paste, find and replace, sort, filter, and format data. You can also meet the format painter and other clipboard functions.

With the front ribbon, you can get font tools to tweak your font, like font name and size, font color, fill color, alignment, wrap text, merge & center, number ribbon for numerical & non-numerical figures, formatting styles, the cell ribbon, and editing ribbon.

Commands

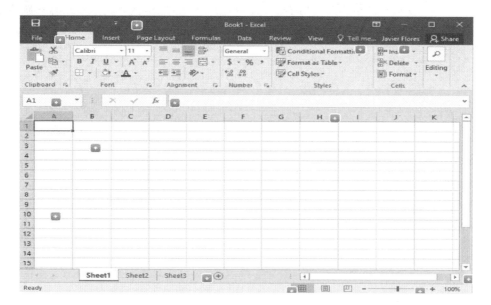

Commands belong to a group.

Name Box

The Name Box allows you to examine the reference (address) for a single cell or range of cells and set the name for that cell or range of cells.

Functions to Insert

It obtains the desired outcome using a particular function depending on its inputs. It is one of Excel's features.

Formula Bar

You may inspect and alter the function or formula that applies to any cell in the sheet for any calculation in the Formula bar.

The resizable bar above the columns of an Excel sheet is known as the formula bar. For better graphics, everything we enter in any cell shows above it. It's excellent for formatting formulae before pressing Enter.

The junction box on its left is where you pick the kind of functions you wish to perform. For example, let's say you're looking for the average (mean), lowest (MIN), or highest (MAX) numerical values in a batch of data.

The name box is located to the left. It shows and informs you of the cell you're in, such as A1.

Row and Column Headings

The column comprises vertical light grey colored lines that carry the letters used to identify each column in a spreadsheet. It has a column header at the top (above the first row). Each row in a worksheet is identified by a group of horizontal light grey colored lines with the number used to identify each row. The Row Heading shows at the top of the page (left of the first column). You can't use Excel's autofill function if you don't have Row and Column Headings.

Vertical/Horizontal Scrollbar

The scrollbar is used to see the worksheet in any area by scrolling up, down, left, or right using the Vertical or Horizontal scrollbar.

Page View Options

Page View Options are located on the right side of the screen, with one on the taskbar.

Normal: It is the default view in the worksheet, and it is simpler to work in this mode.

Page Layout: The worksheet is separated into many page sizes for print preview in Page Layout mode.

Page Break Preview: The Page Break Preview displays the worksheet as individual pages with content to examine how a page appears.

Zoom Slider/Toolbar

Use the Zoom slider, which displays in the bottom right corner of the workbook, to zoom in and out of an excel spreadsheet to the appropriate size.

Select all with a single click

To select the full worksheet, click on the top left of the common area (Under the Name Box) of the Column and Row Headings. Ctrl + A is the same thing.

Gridlines

The Gridlines are a collection of horizontal and vertical light grey colored lines in a worksheet.

Cell

A cell is formed by the intersection of rows and columns in a worksheet.

Cell Address

The column letter identifies a cell's position, while the row number is the cell address or reference.

Active Cell

A bold cell with a black outline is an Active Cell. An active cell is a distinguishable mark that allows you to input and change data.

Sheet tab/active sheet

The name of the sheet tab is bold and shows in the bottom left corner of the workbook while a chosen worksheet is presently being utilized.

Cell range

A range of cells is defined as more than two cells chosen horizontally or vertically in the Microsoft Excel Spreadsheet Environment.

Tabs on sheets

Sheet tabs are the names of the sheets that emerge from the bottom left corner of the worksheet in the Microsoft Excel Spreadsheet Environment.

Insert Tab

The Insert tab is mostly used for visualizing data. Using images, charts, and 3D maps entails bringing your data to life.

Page Layout

This tab is used to set up pages and print them. It controls the worksheet's layout, margins, alignment, and print area.

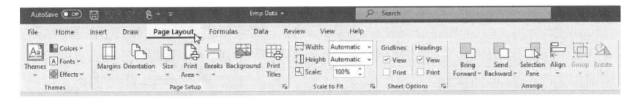

Formulas

This tab allows you to enter functions name variables and change the values of calculation parameters. It is in charge of the computation choices.

Data

This tab includes controls for manipulating worksheet data and connecting to other data sources. In addition, it has features for sorting, filtering, and modifying data.

Review

This tab mainly provides capabilities for verifying spells, documenting changes, making notes and comments, sharing and safeguarding worksheets in Excel workbooks.

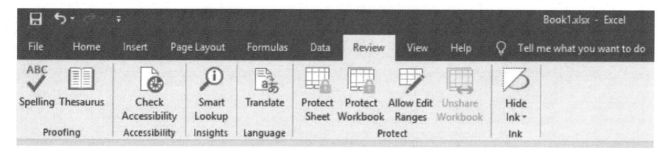

View

Switch between worksheets, see excel worksheets, freeze panes, and organize and manage numerous windows are all available from the View tab.

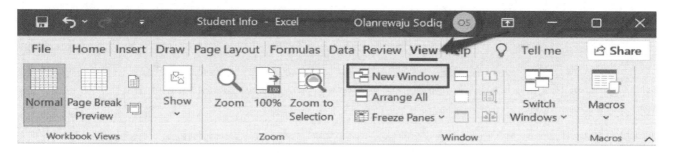

Help

The tab opens the Help Task Pane, where you can search any term and learn more.

The developer is the term for this. The developer tab may be accessed by selecting the File tab, then heading to Options, selecting "Customized Ribbon," selecting the developer option, ticking the box, and clicking OK.

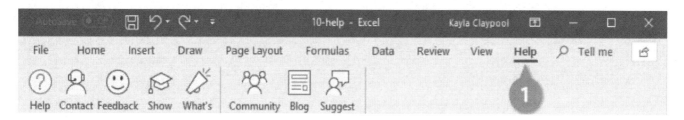

Chapter 4: Getting the Best of Excel Formulas

Formulas in Excel can be a powerful tool that allows you to analyze your data and make predictions.

Most people new to spreadsheet software are not always familiar with formulas and how they come into play, so a few words on this topic might help you understand more about them.

Formulas are used to add or subtract values; they can also perform math operations and calculations. For example, you can use the formula in Excel to create a summary of the information in your spreadsheet. Several functions allow you to make calculations in Excel, for example, SUM(), SUMIF(), or AVERAGE().

Formulas have some hidden features that you might not even realize about them. For example, you can insert a formula in a cell, which will work; however, if you move that cell to another spot in the same spreadsheet, the formula will not correctly reflect the new data.

Defining an Excel Formula

If you're wondering, "What is an Excel Formula?" you've come to the right place. A formula is a mathematical expression used in Excel to perform calculations. It contains standard operators such as a plus sign (+), minus sign (-), backslash (/), asterisk (*), and comma. The information after the equals sign is used to calculate the final value. The formula bar lets you see it as you enter it.

A formula in Excel is an expression that works with values in a range of cells or a single cell. For example, =A1+A2+A3 calculates the sum of cells A1 through A3 values.

Inserting Formulas in Microsoft Excel

The horizontal menu will assist you in finding and inserting formulas into specific cells.

If you are using Microsoft Excel, you may wonder how to insert formulas in the spreadsheet. Excel comes with built-in functions that perform helpful calculations. You can access these functions by clicking on the Insert Function button, the "fx" symbol next to the formula bar. For example, if you want to calculate the area of a city, you can click on cell D2 and the insert function button. The dialogue box will then appear.

A formula will be displayed in the cell where you want it to appear. The formula will be recalculated when the values in the cell change, and the updated answer will appear on the worksheet. This feature is helpful if you want to add or remove specific values. It will be easier to insert a formula if you're familiar with Excel. In addition, you can insert more than one formula in the same cell, which will simplify your work.

The first step in creating a formula is to choose the desired cell in the worksheet. If you're trying to subtract a number from a cell, you should use the '-' sign to make the formula. After this step, you can move on to constructing the formula. After you've decided on a value for your formula, you can then type the remainder of the formula in the next cell, adjusting the cell references accordingly.

In Microsoft Excel, formulas are sometimes known as "functions." To add one to your spreadsheet, pick a cell where a formula is needed and tap the "Insert Function" button on the far left to search for basic formulae and functions. The browser window would look like this:

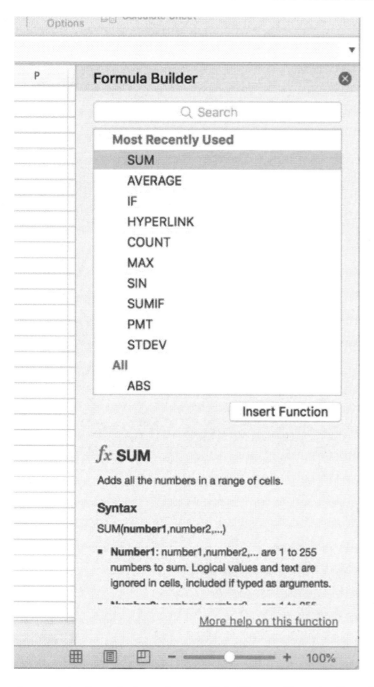

As seen in the window above, click "Insert Function" until you find a formula that works for you.

To insert the formula by Simple Method

To input a formula, follow the steps below.

1. Begin by selecting a cell to work with.

2. Use the equal sign (=) to notify Excel you intend to enter a formula.

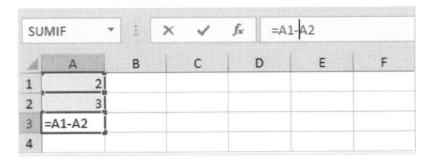

3. As an example, type the formula A1+A2.

4. Change the value of cell A1 to 3.

5. Excel updates the value of column A3 automatically.

To Change a Formula

When you click a cell in Excel, the value or formula of that cell appears in the formula bar.

1. Click on the formula bar and make the required modifications to update a formula.

2. Press the Enter key on your keyboard.

Priority of Operator

The default order in which Excel calculations are conducted is configured. First, it will be calculated if a piece of the formula is included in parentheses. After that, it does multiplication and division calculations. Finally, when you're finished, Excel will add and subtract the remainder of your calculation. Take a look at the example on the right.

To begin, Excel multiplies the values (A1 * A2). Excel then adds the value of column A3 to this result.

How to Create a Formula by Copying and Pasting in MS Excel

If you need to create a formula in MS Excel, you can copy and paste a cell with a formula. When you copy a cell, the reference to the original cell will be preserved. By copying and pasting a cell with a formula, you can easily create a new one with the same formula in a different cell. Moreover, you can also paste a cell with a formula to another column or row.

To copy a single cell, select the cell containing the desired range, then right-click and choose Copy. Next, you can press CTRL + C or click the Paste Options button using a keyboard. Alternatively, you can use the Paste icon in a different column. After copying a cell, click on the paste icon and paste the range into Column F. If there are reference data gaps, you must repeat the copying process.

Another method to copy a cell value is to press Control+D or Control+Shift+'. When copying a cell, you can choose to copy the contents of the cell or just paste the formatting. For example, using Control+C and Control+V will allow you to copy and paste a cell into another cell. You can also copy a cell with a range of cells.

On copying, the cell references for each cell where you copy the formula change automatically.

To obtain a better grasp of this, do the tasks listed below.

1. In cell A4, enter the following formula.

A4			×	✓	f_x	=A1*(A2+A3)	

	A	B	C	D	E	F
1	2	5				
2	2	6				
3	1	4				
4	6					
5						

2a. Right-click cell A4, then choose Copy and Paste from the 'Paste Options menu.

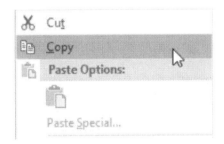

2b. You may drag the formula to cell B4 and drop it there. Cell A4 is chosen, and its bottom right corner is clicked and dragged to cell B4. It's a lot less work and yields the same result!

A4			×	✓	f_x	=A1*(A2+A3)	

	A	B	C	D	E	F
1	2	5				
2	2	6				
3	1	4				
4	6					
5						

Result. In cell B4, the formula refers to the numbers in column B.

B4			✕	✓	*fx*	=B1*(B2+B3)	
◢	A	B	C	D	E	F	
1	2	5					
2	2	6					
3	1	4					
4	6	50					
5							

Using the Basic Formulas in Excel

The formulae in this section are for Microsoft Excel 2022. Therefore, some of the functions listed below may be at a different location if you're using an earlier version of MS Excel.

You're probably wondering how to use the most common formulas in Microsoft Excel. Here's a quick overview of the most popular formulas in Excel. Before creating a formula, you must first enter an equal sign in the cells you want to add or subtract.

The spreadsheet application is easy when you know how to enter data into rows and columns. Then, you can enter mathematical calculations by using the formulas and functions that come with Excel. These calculations can be very useful in business and education, where trend results are significant. With the power of Excel, the possibilities are virtually endless.

1. SUM

The equals sign, =, is utilized in all Microsoft Excel formulae and a text tag expressing the formula you want Microsoft Excel to perform.

In MS Excel, the SUM formula is one of the most used formulae for finding the sum or total of two or more numbers in a spreadsheet.

To use the SUM formula, enter the numbers you wish to add together in the format =SUM (value 1, value 2, and so on).

Real numbers or the value of a specific cell in your spreadsheet may be entered into the SUM function.

Write the following formula in a cell to determine the SUM of 30 and 80, for example, =SUM (40, 80). Then, when you hit "Enter," the cell displays the sum of the two numbers: 120.

Write the following formula in a cell to get the total values in B2 and B11, for example, =SUM (B2, B11). The cell will compute the sum of the integers in cells B2 and B11 when you hit "Enter." If neither cell has any numbers, the formula will yield zero.

Remember that you can get the cumulative sum of an integer list using Microsoft Excel. To determine the total numbers in cells B2 through B11, use the following formula in a spreadsheet cell: =TOTAL (B2:B11). In every cell, there is a colon instead of a comma. Here's how it may look in a Microsoft Excel spreadsheet for a content marketer:

SUM		✕ ✓ ƒx	=SUM(B2:B11)		

	A	B	C	D
1	Source of views	Generated Leads		
2	Blog post #1	10		
3	Blog post #2	4		
4	Blog post #3	3		
5	Blog post #4	13		
6	Blog post #5	14		
7	Blog post #6	7		
8	Blog post #7	6		
9	Blog post #8	9		
10	Blog post #9	18		
11	Blog post #10	3		
12		=SUM(B2:B11)		
13				

2. The Average

Simple averages of data should come to mind when using the AVERAGE function.

=AVERAGE (num1, [num2],)

SUM		✕ ✓ ƒx	=AVERAGE(B2:B11)		

	A	B	C	D
1	Country	2022 Population		
2	China	1,425,887,337		
3	India	1,417,173,173		
4	United States	338,289,857		
5	Indonesia	275,501,339		
6	Pakistan	235,824,862		
7	Nigeria	218,541,212		
8	Brazil	215,313,498		
9	Bangladesh	171,186,372		
10	Russia	144,713,314		
11	Mexico	127,504,125		
12		=AVERAGE(B2:B11)		
13				
14				

3. COUNT

This counts the number of cells within a range that solely contains numeric values. It is written as

=COUNT (1st value, [2nd value],)

Example:

COUNT (B: B) – Counts all numerical values in column B. To count rows, you must change the range within the calculation.

COUNT (B1:D1) – It now counts rows within the given range.

4. COUNTA

It counts all cells in a range. It does, however, count all cells, but the cell kind is ignored. Unlike COUNT, which only counts numerics, this function counts strings, empty strings, dates, logical values, times, text, and errors.

=COUNTA (1st value, [2nd value2] ....etc.)

Example:

COUNTA (C13:C2) However, unlike COUNT, you can't count rows using the same algorithm. COUNTA (H2:C2), for example, will count columns C to H if you change the selection within the brackets.

COUNTA	✕ ✓ fx	=COUNTA(B2:B13)
	A	B	C
1	Country	2022 Population	
2	China	1,425,887,337	
3	India	1,417,173,173	
4	United States	338,289,857	
5	Indonesia	275,501,339	
6		Empty	
7	Pakistan	235,824,862	
8	Nigeria	218,541,212	
9			
10	Brazil	215,313,498	
11	Bangladesh	171,186,372	
12	Russia	144,713,314	
13	Mexico	127,504,125	
14	COUNTA	=COUNTA(B2:B13)	
15			

	A	B	C
1	Country	2022 Population	
2	China	1,425,887,337	
3	India	1,417,173,173	
4	United States	338,289,857	
5	Indonesia	275,501,339	
6		Empty	
7	Pakistan	235,824,862	
8	Nigeria	218,541,212	
9			
10	Brazil	215,313,498	
11	Bangladesh	171,186,372	
12	Russia	144,713,314	
13	Mexico	127,504,125	
14	COUNTA	11	
15			
16			

5. IF Statement

This sorts data according to certain rules. This formula includes formulae and functions.

=IF(logical test, [value if true], [value if false])

Example:

=IF(D3<C3, 'TRUE,' 'FALSE') =IF(D3C3, 'TRUE,' 'FALSE') – If the value at C3 is smaller than the value at D3, the condition is true. If the reasoning is correct, set the cell value to TRUE; otherwise, set it to FALSE.

=IF(SUM(F10:F1) > SUM(G10:G1 – A complicated IF logic example. It adds F1 to F10 and G1 to G10 first, then compares the results. When the total of F1 to G10 exceeds the summation of G1 to G10, the cell's value becomes equal to F1 to F10. Otherwise, the SUM of F1 through F10 is calculated.

C22	× ✓ fx		

	A	B	C	D
1	**Country**	**2022 Population**	**Average Population**	**Greater than Average?**
2	China	1,425,887,337	456,993,509	TRUE
3	India	1,417,173,173	456,993,509	TRUE
4	United States	338,289,857	456,993,509	FALSE
5	Indonesia	275,501,339	456,993,509	FALSE
6	Pakistan	235,824,862	456,993,509	FALSE
7	Nigeria	218,541,212	456,993,509	FALSE
8	Brazil	215,313,498	456,993,509	FALSE
9	Bangladesh	171,186,372	456,993,509	FALSE
10	Russia	144,713,314	456,993,509	FALSE
11	Mexico	127,504,125	456,993,509	FALSE
12				

6. TRIM

Using the TRIM feature, it is possible to prevent disorganized areas from interfering with your daily activities. That there are no open slots is ensured by this method. However, when TRIM is used, it only affects a single cell instead of other activities that may affect a group of cells. Therefore, it has the issue of reproducing data on your spreadsheet, which is a disadvantage.

=TRIM(text)

For Instance:

TRIM(A2) – extract empty spaces from cell A2's value.

B2	× ✓ fx	=TRIM(A2)

	A	B
1	**Raw Data**	**TRIM**
2	China 2022	China 2022
3	2021 India	2021 India
4	United States 2022	United States 2022
5	Indonesia 2021	Indonesia 2021
6	Pakistan 2023	Pakistan 2023
7	Nigeria 2025	Nigeria 2025
8	Brazil 2021	Brazil 2021
9	Bangladesh 2020	Bangladesh 2020
10	Russia 2019	Russia 2019
11	Mexico 2018	Mexico 2018
12		

7. MAXIMUM AND MINIMUM

The maximum and minimum functions assist in determining the maximum and minimum values within a series of values.

MINIMUM

=MIN(value1, [value2],...)

MAXIMUM

=MAX(integer1, [interger2],...)

MIN | × ✓ fx | =MIN(B2:B11)

	A	B	C
1	Country	2022 Population	Average Population
2	China	1,425,887,337	456,993,509
3	India	1,417,173,173	456,993,509
4	United States	338,289,857	456,993,509
5	Indonesia	275,501,339	456,993,509
6	Pakistan	235,824,862	456,993,509
7	Nigeria	218,541,212	456,993,509
8	Brazil	215,313,498	456,993,509
9	Bangladesh	171,186,372	456,993,509
10	Russia	144,713,314	456,993,509
11	Mexico	127,504,125	456,993,509
12		=MIN(B2:B11)	
13			
14			
15			

MAX | × ✓ fx | =MAX(B2:B11)

	A	B	C
1	Country	2022 Population	Average Population
2	China	1,425,887,337	456,993,509
3	India	1,417,173,173	456,993,509
4	United States	338,289,857	456,993,509
5	Indonesia	275,501,339	456,993,509
6	Pakistan	235,824,862	456,993,509
7	Nigeria	218,541,212	456,993,509
8	Brazil	215,313,498	456,993,509
9	Bangladesh	171,186,372	456,993,509
10	Russia	144,713,314	456,993,509
11	Mexico	127,504,125	456,993,509
12		=MAX(B2:B11)	
13			

8. Percentage

Type =A1/B1 into the cells where you wish to find a percentage to utilize the formula in Excel Spreadsheets. To convert a decimal number to a %, select the cell, go to the Home tab, and choose "Percentage" from the digits menu.

Although Microsoft Excel doesn't have a "formula" for percentages, it does make it easy to convert the value of any cell to a %, so you don't have to waste time measuring and reentering the numbers.

The particular option for converting the value of a cell to a percentage may be found on Microsoft Excel's Home tab. First, choose Conditional Formatting from the drop-down menu next to this column, then highlight the cell(s) you wish to convert to a percent (this menu tab might say "General" first).

Then choose "Percentage" from the drop-down menu that appears. Each cell you've marked will have its meaning transformed into a percentage. You will find it a little farther down the page.

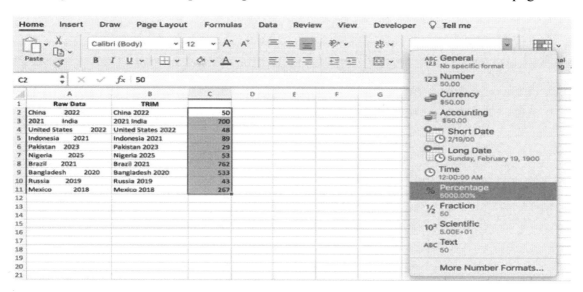

Remember that the results will default to decimals if you use other formulae to produce new numbers, such as the division formula (notated =A1/B1). Before or after applying this method, select the cells and change their format to "Percentage" using the home tab, as seen above.

9. Subtraction

To run the subtraction algorithm in Microsoft Excel, enter the cells you want to subtract in the format =SUM (A1, -B1). You may use the SUM formula to subtract it by putting a negative sign directly before the cell you're removing. For example, if A1 is 10 and B1 is 6, =SUM(A1, -B1) produces 4 instead of 10 + -6.

In MS Excel, subtracting, including fractions, lacks a formula, but that doesn't imply it can't be done. There are two methods for removing particular values (or inside cells).

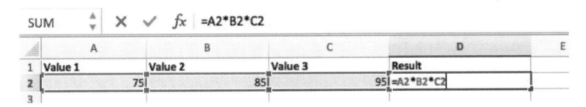

=SUM was used as a formula. In the layout =SUM(A1, -B1), enter the cells you wish to subtract, with the minus sign (denoted by a hyphen) directly before the cell whose value you want to remove. Enter to find the distance between the two parenthesis cells. Look at the image above to get a sense of how this works.

In the format, write =A1-B1. To subtract several values from each other, enter an equal sign, the first value or cell, a hyphen, and then the value to be subtracted. Finally, enter to obtain the difference between the two numbers.

10. Multiplication

Insert the cells for multiplying in Microsoft Excel format =A1*B1 to run the multiplication formula. This formula uses an asterisk to multiply cell A1 by cell B1. For example, if A1 is 10 and B1 is 6, the result of =A1*B1 is 60.

You could think that multiplying values in MS Excel has a formula or that the "x" character signifies multiple multiplied values.

Using an asterisk — * — is all it takes.

Mark an empty cell in an MS Excel spreadsheet to multiply two or more numbers. Then, in the format =A1*B1*C1..., put the numbers or cells you want to multiply together in the format =A1*B1*C1... The asterisk would effectively double each meaning in the calculation.

Press Enter to return your preferred item. To show how this works, check the screenshot above.

11. Division

In MS Excel, put =F1/G1 into the cells you wish to divide to utilize the division formula. The forward slash, "/," splits cell F1 by cell G1. For example, if F1 is 10 and G1 is 20, =F1/G1 returns 0.5 as a decimal number.

Division is one of the most fundamental functions in Microsoft Excel. To do so, open a new cell and write "=," followed by the two (or more) values you wish to divide, separated by a forward dash, "/." The result should be in the format =B2/A2, as seen in the image below.

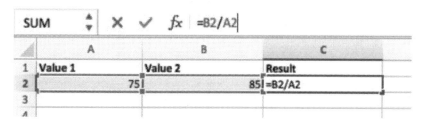

When you hit Enter, the highlighted cell will display your selected quotient.

12. DATE TIME

The MS Excel DATE formula is DATE =DATE (year, month, day). This formula will provide a date that matches the data in the brackets and values from other cells. For example, if A1 is 2018, B1 is 7, and C1 is 11, =DATE(A1,B1,C1) returns 7/11/2018.

It might be tough to input dates into the cells of a Microsoft Excel database at times. Fortunately, formatting dates is easy using a simple formula. This formula can be used in two different ways:

To make dates, use a series of cell values. Select an empty cell, enter "=DATE," and then put the values of the cells that make up your chosen date in parentheses, starting with the year, month number, and ending with the day. DATE= (year, month, day). To show how this works, check the screenshot below.

Set a date for today automatically. Select an empty cell and enter =DATE(YEAR(TODAY()), MONTH(TODAY()), DAY(TODAY()) in it. The most recent date in your MS Excel spreadsheet will be returned if you click enter.

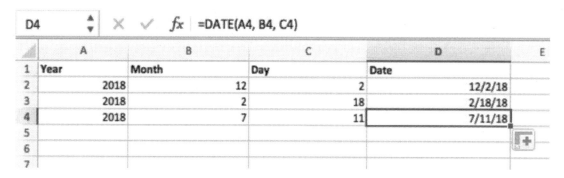

Assume your Microsoft Excel program is set up differently. When utilizing the date formula in Microsoft Excel, your returned date must be in the format "mm/dd/yy."

13. Match

To use the MATCH formula in Microsoft Excel, first select a list. Then type the string to be matched. This function will return an error if the result is an empty string. This error indicates that no match was found. If your data isn't sorted in the order you entered it, then type a search in the first column of the data set. The second column will return the position of the value matched by the MATCH function.

When using the MS Excel MATCH formula, you can search for a specific value in a column. For example, if a value is present in cell G2, the MATCH formula will return that value from A2 to A9. For a specific array, you can use the INDEX function, which returns a single value in a range by comparing the position of that value against the number in the column. In addition, the INDEX formula takes into account the relative row number.

To check the position for 62:

A9	fx	=MATCH(62, A1:A7, 0)

	A	B	C	D	E
1	540				
2	23				
3	45				
4	62				
5	45				
6	34				
7	72				
8					
9	4				

Checking the position for 69 will bring an error displayed as #N/A:

A9	fx	=MATCH(69, A1:A7, 0)

	A	B	C	D	E
1	540				
2	23				
3	45				
4	62				
5	45				
6	34				
7	72				
8					
9	#N/A				
10					

The MATCH function results in an error

There are three main ways to use the Match Formula in MS Excel. The first is to use a 'number' as the lookup value. This allows you to search for numbers or text within a cell easily. The second method uses a 'text' value, which works like a regular cell reference. These two methods are used to search for strings in documents and spreadsheets. The first method allows you to specify the match type, also known as 'text,' and the second approach uses a "reference" to return the value.

Another way to use the Match Function in MS Excel is by creating a lookup table. You can also use the INDEX function to locate specific values within a list. The INDEX function returns the value in a particular column and gives you its reference in the same position in the other column. To create a lookup table in MS Excel, use the "JK002" as the first parameter. The INDEX function will return a value with the same name as the number in column A.

14. How to Use the VLOOKUP Function in MS Excel

The VLOOKUP function in MS Excel allows you to look up specific information about a particular item. For example, this feature will enable you to enter the details of a particular item, such as a specific grade, and find out if that grade has already been assigned to another item. VLOOKUP can also look up a single item from an inventory list. The following steps will guide you through the process. If you are unfamiliar with VLOOKUP, you can use a short video to get an overview.

First, identify the column you'd like to fill in. Next, select the Functions tab and choose VLOOKUP. You can then type the formula into the highlighted cell. In addition, you can type the lookup value and column number into the formula. Once you've done this, click the "Done" button. This will populate the first cell. You can also check the value of your VLOOKUP formula by clicking the tiny square on the bottom right corner of the cell.

When using VLOOKUP, you should be careful with your input value. The lookup value can be a number or a text string. If it's a number, you don't need to use quotes; the default value is TRUE. The range_lookup parameter specifies whether the lookup value must be exact or approximate. If it's not, you can specify an approximate match.

E2		fx	=VLOOKUP(E1, A2:B7, 2, FALSE)		
	A	B	C	D	E	F
1	Animal	Speed(mph)		Animal	Antelope	
2	Cheetah	70		Speed	61	
3	Zebra	59				
4	Antelope	61				
5	Lion	50				
6	Elk	45				
7	Coyote	43				
8						

15. Financial Formulas

Financial formulas calculate financial transactions using money values, such as interest rates and percentages. To learn how to write financial formulas in Excel, you will need to know how to use some formulas that operate with these values.

16. How to Use the Random Numbers Generator in Microsoft Excel

This section will show you how to use the Random numbers generator in Microsoft Excel to generate random numbers for your data. This is an analytics tool that you can use to find out patterns. Its various options include a lower and an upper limit, step, and repetition rate for both values and sequence. You can even sort the results using a column. In the end, the sum of probabilities should equal one. But it's not as simple as that. There are more sophisticated options for Excel.

First, choose the range you wish to use to generate random numbers. You can either select a range of cells or specify a pre-selected range. Excel will generate a new one if you don't specify a range. If you select a specific range, the generated data will overwrite the existing data. Next, choose the New Worksheet Ply option to insert a new worksheet within the current workbook. You can then paste the random data into cell A1 in the first sheet. After completing this step, press the OK button.

You can use the formula:

=rand() or

=randbetween(minimum_value,max_value)

Once you have created the ranges, you can use the formula to generate random numbers. To find out how many numbers are in each category, enter the formula for round down in cell E1. After the formula, you should see a chart with a normal distribution. Ideally, this chart will resemble a bell shape.

Chapter 5: Excel for Beginners

When you apply your knowledge of Microsoft Excel to production data, you can create a simple chart or graph that is easy for users to understand. This means you will better grasp what you see in your spreadsheet, which is essential because it means fewer errors when producing your report. So now that we've got that out of the way, how do we get started?

Frequently Used Tasks added to Your Toolbar

You may wonder how to add frequently used tasks to the toolbar in Microsoft Office. There are several ways to customize your toolbar in Excel, including moving it below or above the ribbon and customizing the order of the commands. For example, you may add your favorites to the Quick Access Toolbar instead of scrolling between the various tabs of the ribbon every time.

Microsoft has various options for doing so, but the simplest is to right-click on the item you wish to add and choose "Add to Quick Access Toolbar."

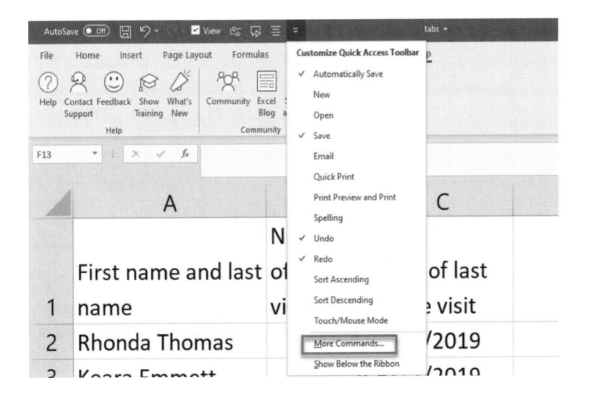

You can rearrange your QAT shortcuts to suit your needs.

Filter your Data

Filtering data is one of the easiest ways to find specific pieces of information. The Sort & Filter feature is essential in dealing with data. Filters can be applied to the entire column or just to individual rows. To filter specific data, select the data you want to filter. Then, on the Home ribbon, select the Sort & Filter option. The data will now be filtered and displayed.

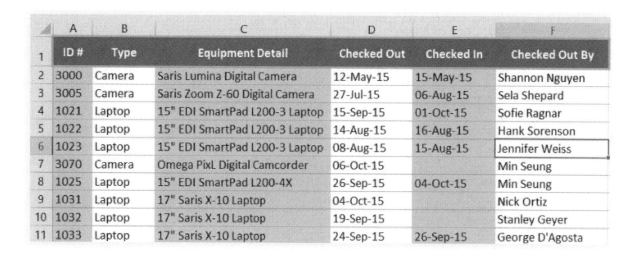

	A	B	C	D	E	F
1	ID #	Type	Equipment Detail	Checked Out	Checked In	Checked Out By
2	3000	Camera	Saris Lumina Digital Camera	12-May-15	15-May-15	Shannon Nguyen
3	3005	Camera	Saris Zoom Z-60 Digital Camera	27-Jul-15	06-Aug-15	Sela Shepard
4	1021	Laptop	15" EDI SmartPad L200-3 Laptop	15-Sep-15	01-Oct-15	Sofie Ragnar
5	1022	Laptop	15" EDI SmartPad L200-3 Laptop	14-Aug-15	16-Aug-15	Hank Sorenson
6	1023	Laptop	15" EDI SmartPad L200-3 Laptop	08-Aug-15	15-Aug-15	Jennifer Weiss
7	3070	Camera	Omega PixL Digital Camcorder	06-Oct-15		Min Seung
8	1025	Laptop	15" EDI SmartPad L200-4X	26-Sep-15	04-Oct-15	Min Seung
9	1031	Laptop	17" Saris X-10 Laptop	04-Oct-15		Nick Ortiz
10	1032	Laptop	17" Saris X-10 Laptop	19-Sep-15		Stanley Geyer
11	1033	Laptop	17" Saris X-10 Laptop	24-Sep-15	26-Sep-15	George D'Agosta

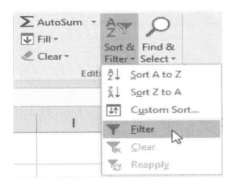

Click the drop-down arrow for the column you want to filter. In our example, we will filter column B to view only certain types of equipment.

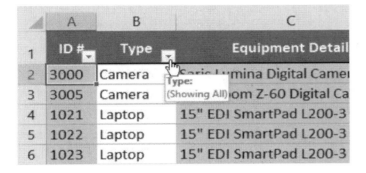

Uncheck the box next to Select All to quickly deselect all data.

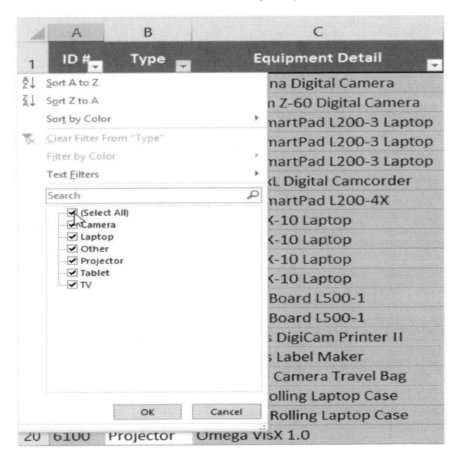

Check the boxes next to the data you want to filter, then click OK. In this example, we will check Laptop and Projector to view only these types of equipment.

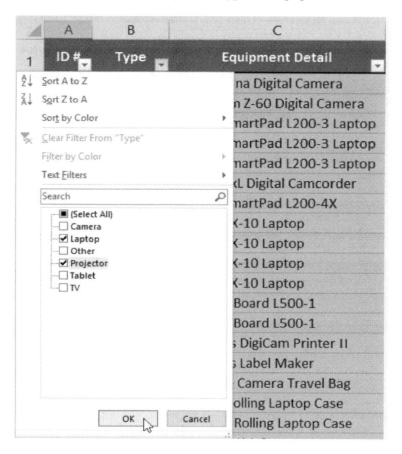

The data will be filtered, temporarily hiding any content that doesn't match the criteria. In our example, only laptops and projectors are visible.

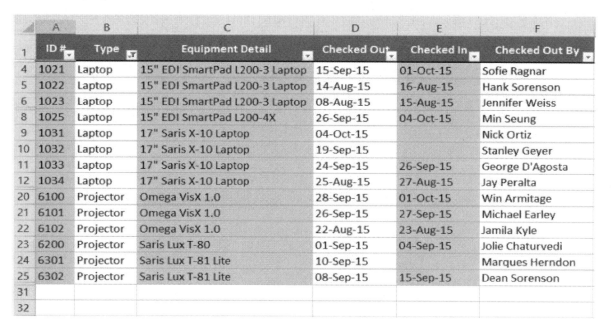

	A	B	C	D	E	F
1	ID #	Type	Equipment Detail	Checked Out	Checked In	Checked Out By
4	1021	Laptop	15" EDI SmartPad L200-3 Laptop	15-Sep-15	01-Oct-15	Sofie Ragnar
5	1022	Laptop	15" EDI SmartPad L200-3 Laptop	14-Aug-15	16-Aug-15	Hank Sorenson
6	1023	Laptop	15" EDI SmartPad L200-3 Laptop	08-Aug-15	15-Aug-15	Jennifer Weiss
8	1025	Laptop	15" EDI SmartPad L200-4X	26-Sep-15	04-Oct-15	Min Seung
9	1031	Laptop	17" Saris X-10 Laptop	04-Oct-15		Nick Ortiz
10	1032	Laptop	17" Saris X-10 Laptop	19-Sep-15		Stanley Geyer
11	1033	Laptop	17" Saris X-10 Laptop	24-Sep-15	26-Sep-15	George D'Agosta
12	1034	Laptop	17" Saris X-10 Laptop	25-Aug-15	27-Aug-15	Jay Peralta
20	6100	Projector	Omega VisX 1.0	28-Sep-15	01-Oct-15	Win Armitage
21	6101	Projector	Omega VisX 1.0	26-Sep-15	27-Sep-15	Michael Earley
22	6102	Projector	Omega VisX 1.0	22-Aug-15	23-Aug-15	Jamila Kyle
23	6200	Projector	Saris Lux T-80	01-Sep-15	04-Sep-15	Jolie Chaturvedi
24	6301	Projector	Saris Lux T-81 Lite	10-Sep-15		Marques Herndon
25	6302	Projector	Saris Lux T-81 Lite	08-Sep-15	15-Sep-15	Dean Sorenson
31						
32						

The use of dynamic headers and footers

Embedding headers and footers are relatively simple. Headers are usually displayed only on printed pages. You can view headers and footers by selecting the Page Layout view option on the Insert menu. Next, select the appropriate cell and type the text into the Header box to create a header. If you don't want headers, leave the text inside the worksheet. To add a footer, select the same process as adding a header.

You can easily add a header and footer to a table. For example, adding the current date and adjusted date to a header is easy with a macro. You can also add a page number to the footer. In addition to adding headers and footers, you can add page numbers to a worksheet. By following these steps, you can easily create attractive reports and make your job easier.

Adding page numbers, timestamps, and file locations to the header or footer is one of the finest methods to maintain track of what's printed out of Excel. In addition, you may include formulae that update automatically to ensure that you don't have to change these values every time you print a spreadsheet.

To begin, alter the view of Excel so that the header and footer are visible.

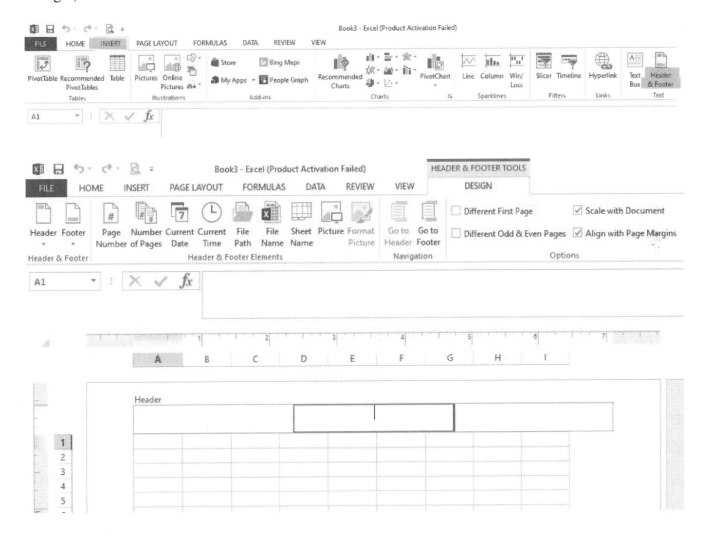

Then, in your header footer, add the following text.

For changes to take effect, click anywhere on the worksheet.

Your print sections

You must first define a print region in Excel to separate columns and rows. To define the print area, click the Page Break Preview button at the bottom right corner of the application. In the print preview, you will see a line around the cell you want to print. Click the cell and set a specific area to print. Only the cells you select will appear on the paper. A light border will appear around the selected cells.

Defining print regions in Microsoft Excel is quite simple. Simply select a range of cells in your workbook, click the Page Layout tab in the ribbon, click the Print Area tool, and select Set Print Area. You can also change the named range Print_Area by clicking the Edit button. Similarly, you can also clear print areas by clicking on the worksheet. Then, print your workbook.

Highlight the cells you wish to print to determine your print area—Select Set Print Area from the drop-down menu under Print Area on the Page Layout ribbon.

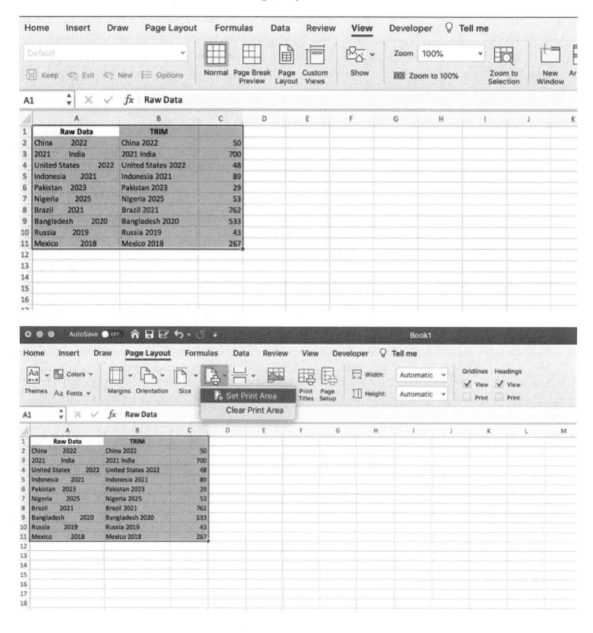

The option to clear the print area is also included in the same drop-down menu. It is a good option if you've altered your spreadsheet and want to expand the printed space.

Paste Special option

The right-click menu contains six Paste Special options: Paste Values, Paste Formulas, Transpose, Formats, and Create Links. Hover over these options to see all 15 types. These options let you selectively copy and paste a range of data. For example, you can select multiple cells if you have too many columns or rows to copy. This can be useful if you need to change the order of data in a table or graph.

The Paste Special option is available in Excel in three places: the ribbon, the right-click menu, and the keyboard shortcuts. You can paste values into one cell or a range of cells. To copy data into another cell, click the cell and then click the clipboard icon. Next, select the data you want to copy and paste and click OK. You can also copy and paste an entire worksheet. Here's how.

The first option is Paste Values. This will paste values without formatting. For example, you can paste formulas without formatting. This option will remove the formatting and paste the values appearing in the cell. You can also select a location for the pasted data. You can also select the Paste Special options if you want to use them more frequently. However, it will cost you a bit of time and patience.

Copy your data as normal, but instead of using Ctrl + V, right-click and choose Paste Special from the menu.

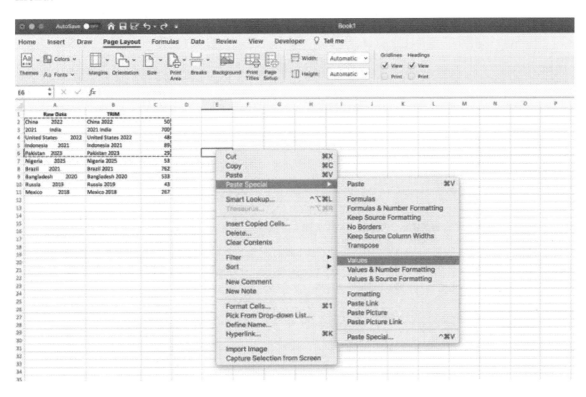

Grouping and ungrouping columns to hide extensive data

Spreadsheets containing many sophisticated and extensive data may be challenging to understand and evaluate. Fortunately, Excel makes it simple to collapse and extend complex details, resulting in a more compact and readable display.

The ideal spreadsheets for grouping in Excel are those with column headers, no blank rows or columns, and data sorted by at least one column.

In the group, choose all of the data you wish to summarize. Then choose Subtotal from the Data tab. It will provide a pop-up window to choose how you want the data to be organized and summarized. For example, we categorized by Order Year change and totaled on Total in the example below. It will show us the total sales for each year and the whole period.

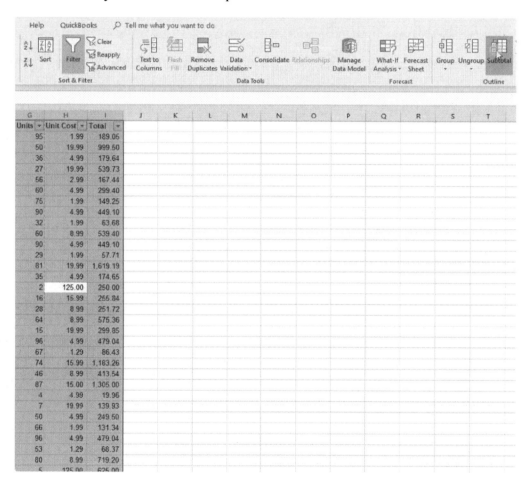

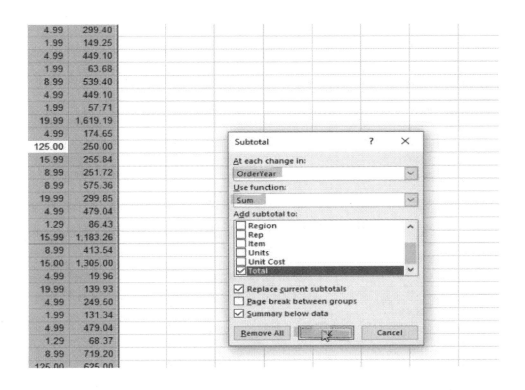

Here is the result:

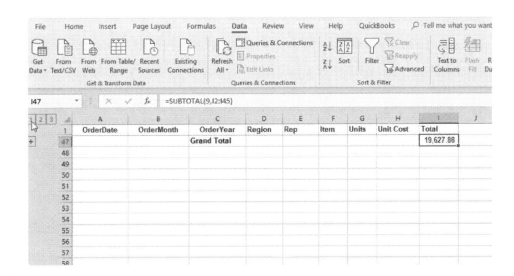

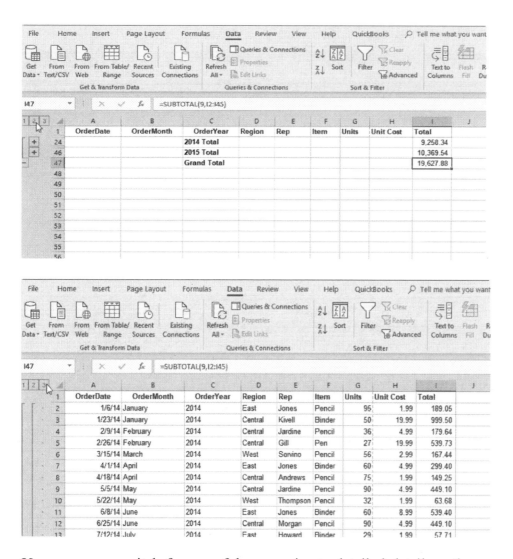

You may now switch from useful summaries to detailed detail on the same spreadsheet with only a few clicks.

Safety of the spreadsheet and workbook

To protect your workbook and documents, you can use password protection. This option allows you to create a secure password that will prevent others from viewing your workbook or altering it. Password protection is case-sensitive, so choose a password that you will not be embarrassed to share with others. Suppose you are worried that someone will try to open the workbook without your permission. In that case, you can remove the password protection or change the password to something less secure.

To protect your workbook from unauthorized changes, you should encrypt it. This will prevent other users from adding or deleting worksheets, hiding sheets, or renaming them.

Excel contains built-in security safeguards to keep your spreadsheets safe.

Click the Review tab on the ribbon, then Protect Workbook to protect a workbook. It will open a pop-up window to enter the unlock password and choose which functionalities people may still access while the Sheet is protected.

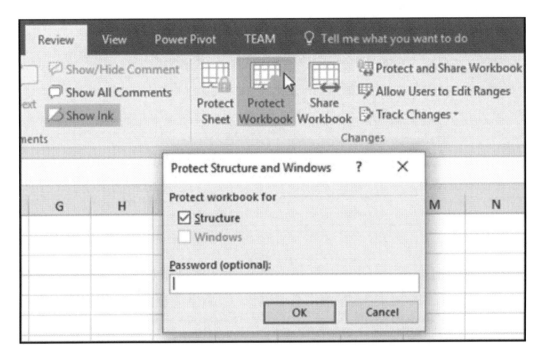

After clicking Ok, you'll be required to confirm the password and save the worksheet. If somebody attempts to change the data, they'll need that password. If you wish to safeguard a group of sheets, click Protect Workbook and follow the same steps.

Tracing precedents and dependents

If you're new to working with formulas and functions in Microsoft Excel, you may want to know how to search for precedents and dependent formulations. This feature will show you the cell references of precedents and dependent formulas and a history of their connections between cells.

Suppose you need to alter the formulae and functions but aren't sure what other calculations will be impacted. In that case, you might waste a lot of time in the spreadsheet with no results. But on the other hand, you can search for a mistake and know where the data is coming from.

With Trace Precedents and Trace Dependents, Excel makes it easy to see which cells are reliant on others and which cells contribute to others.

Both actions are limited to the cell that is now active; as a result, only one cell may be worked on at a time. To generate the blue arrows, it is necessary to use the Trace Precedents or Trace Dependents buttons located in the Formula Auditing section on the Formulas page. This diagram shows data flow, with the blue dot indicating the antecedent and the arrow symbolizing the dependence of the flow.

Cell C2's Trace Dependents reveal that it solely flows to cell E2.

	A	B	C	D	E	F
1	**Raw Data**	**TRIM**			**Totals**	
2	China 2022	China 2022	50	2		
3	2021 India	2021 India	700	5	3500	
4	United States 2022	United States 2022	48	6	288	
5	Indonesia 2021	Indonesia 2021	89	7	623	
6	Pakistan 2023	Pakistan 2023	29	8	232	
7	Nigeria 2025	Nigeria 2025	53	3	159	
8	Brazil 2021	Brazil 2021	762	9	6858	
9	Bangladesh 2020	Bangladesh 2020	533	6	3198	
10	Russia 2019	Russia 2019	43	2	86	
11	Mexico 2018	Mexico 2018	267	4	1068	
12						
13						
14						
15						
16						

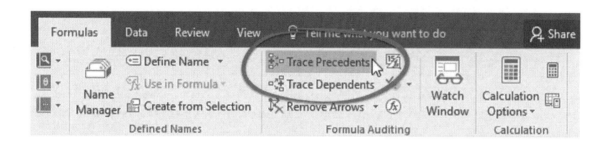

ACCORDING TO TRACE PRECEDENTS, Cell C2 and D2 are the sole cells flowing to cell G4.

| G4 | | $\times$ ✓ fx | =C2*D2 | | | | | |

	A	B	C	D	E	F	G	H
1	**Raw Data**	**TRIM**			**Totals**			
2	China 2022	China 2022	50	2				
3	2021 India	2021 India	700	5	3500			
4	United States 2022	United States 2022	48	6	288		100	
5	Indonesia 2021	Indonesia 2021	89	7	623			
6	Pakistan 2023	Pakistan 2023	29	8	232			
7	Nigeria 2025	Nigeria 2025	53	3	159			
8	Brazil 2021	Brazil 2021	762	9	6858			
9	Bangladesh 2020	Bangladesh 2020	533	6	3198			
10	Russia 2019	Russia 2019	43	2	86			
11	Mexico 2018	Mexico 2018	267	4	1068			
12								
13								
14								
15								
16								

These functionalities operate across tabs of the same worksheet and separate workbooks with one exception. External workbook links will not function with Trace Dependents until they are open.

Data Validation in drop-down menus of a cell

The drop-down list is a terrific way to show your Excel talents to coworkers and employers. Simultaneously, it's a highly user-friendly technique to ensure that bespoke Excel sheets work correctly.

This tool is used to populate a spreadsheet with data based on criteria. Drop-down lists in Excel are mostly used to restrict the number of options accessible to the user. On the other hand, a drop-down menu avoids spelling errors and speeds up data entry.

It also allows you to restrict what may be entered into a cell. As a result, it's ideal for verifying inputs. To begin, go to Ribbon and choose Data and Data Validation.

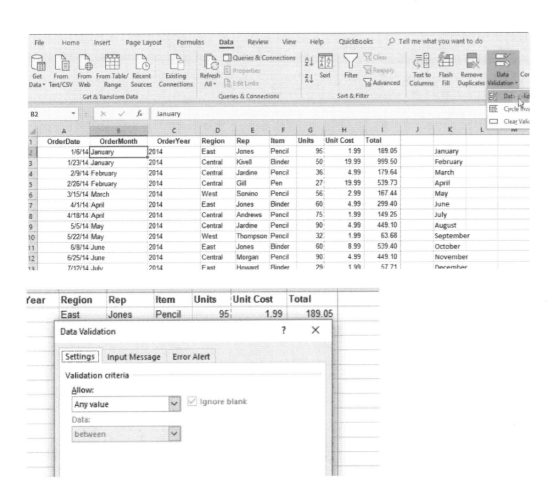

After that, choose your parameters. For example, to fill OrderMonth, we utilized the months of the year.

After clicking Ok, pick from the list by clicking the drop-down arrow adjacent to the cell.

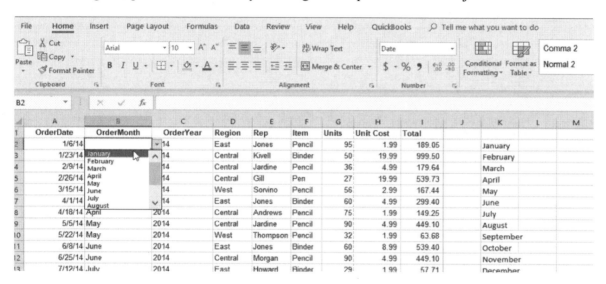

Note that once one cell is set up, it may be copied and pasted into the other cells below.

Working with Text-to-column

This is important in breaking text into new columns. Text to Columns is a quick approach to divide this up since it separates all of the chosen cells simultaneously and places the results in separate columns.

Text to Columns is available in two separate modes: fixed-width and delimited. Delimited divides the text depending on the text, such as every comma, tab, or space, while fixed-width splits the text based on the text, such as every comma, tab, or space.

For example, let's use a delimited Text to Columns to eliminate cents from our total column.

To use Text to Columns, highlight your data and click the Data Ribbon's Text to Columns button. You'll be able to pick between fixed-width and delimited options after you've arrived.

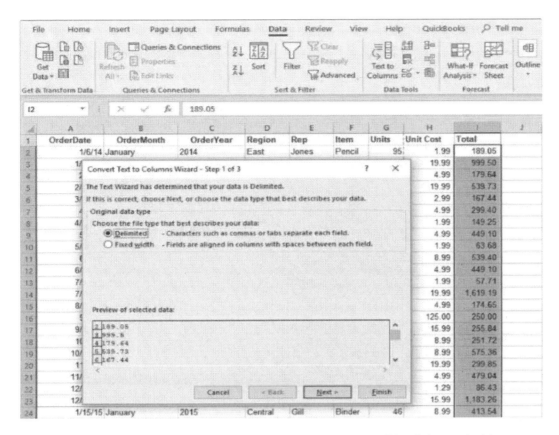

Set your separating criteria on the following screen. We utilized the period in our example.

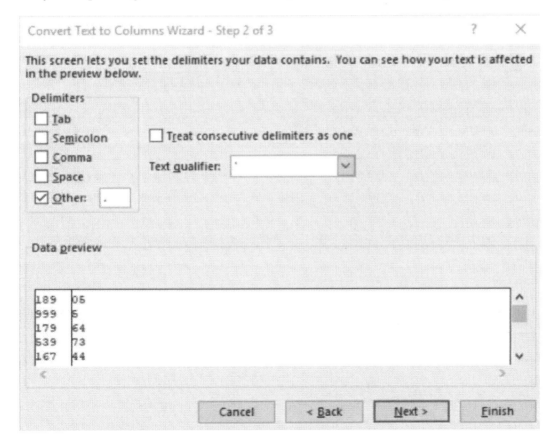

You have the opportunity to omit portions and adjust the formatting on the final screen. It will save you time in the future. After that, click Finish.

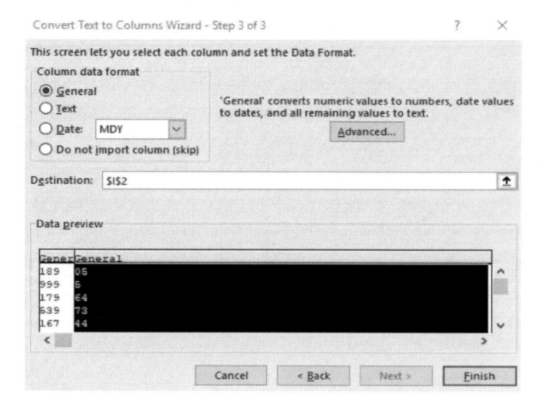

Finally, the outcomes! All of the cents were put in the right-hand column.

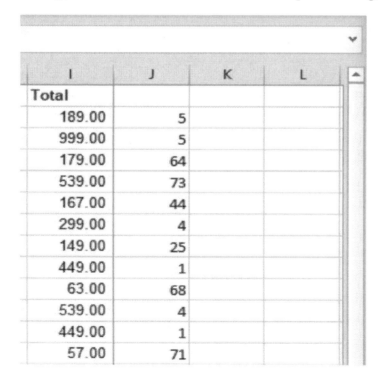

I	J	K	L
Total			
189.00	5		
999.00	5		
179.00	64		
539.00	73		
167.00	44		
299.00	4		
149.00	25		
449.00	1		
63.00	68		
539.00	4		
449.00	1		
57.00	71		

How You Can Make the Graph Using Excel

Although graphs and charts are two different features, Excel groups all graphs into the chart categories mentioned in previous sections; following the steps below, choose the right graph form to generate a graph or another type of chart.

- To make a graph with workbook data, select a range

- By moving your cursor over cells that hold data you want to include in a graph, you will highlight them.

- The greyed-out cell contents will be illuminated.

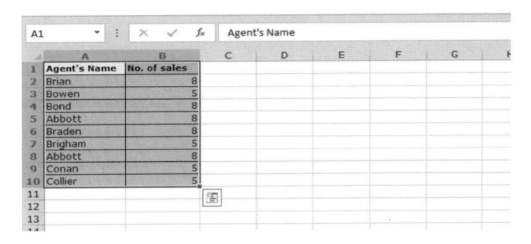

- After the text has been outlined, you can choose a graph (Excel refers to a chart).

- On the toolbar, choose Recommended Charts from your Insert tab. Then choose the graph form you want to use.

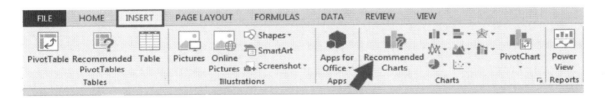

The recommended charts procedure

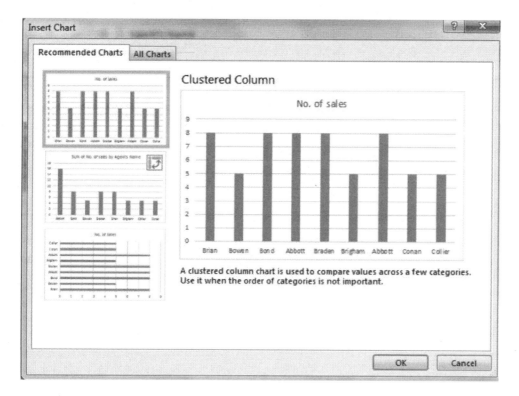

Selecting the graph type

You now have the graph on your screen. To personalize your graph, repeat the measures outlined in the previous section. When making a graph, all the functions for making a chart remain the same.

Chapter 6: Excel for Middle-Level Users

Intermediate skills in Excel are essential to get started using this popular business application. These skills include using Excel keyboard shortcuts, understanding how to enter data into different Excel workbooks, and finding and searching for specific data. Intermediate skills also include using filters and line charts to visually present the final summary of data. Intermediate users can also print their results, which they can use as a reference when making business decisions.

The Enhanced Intermediate skills

Intermediate skills in Excel help you sort and analyze data more efficiently. For example, you can find data and sort it into various worksheets and workbooks. Advanced features help you make sense of complex data. For example, you can use the filter feature and create a line chart to visualize data and present it meaningfully. Intermediate skills in Excel also help you make graphs, tables, and charts. Once you have these skills, you can even print the results.

To test your intermediate Excel skills, try the Excel challenge exercise. This exercise aims to see how much you know about spreadsheet formulas, pivot tables, and data visualization. Completing all ten exercises will help you determine your level of skill. For example, if you completed eight exercises, you have intermediate skills. You can move to the next level if you have some experience with the program. This will help you get more experience using the program.

There are many ways to assess your skill level in Excel. Whether you want to train your staff or want to gauge how much of your learning is sufficient, various online tests are available. You can choose to do an Excel for medium-level users with intermediate skills test or do an online assessment. Regardless of your skill level, the goal is to improve your skills and increase your job opportunities. The skills assessment is a vital part of your job search.

After you've mastered the fundamentals, you'll need to learn about Intermediate Excel Skills. Essentially, these abilities provide alternatives and ways for efficiently managing and working with data.

Using the Special Section

The GO TO SPECIAL option within the worksheet allows you to browse a particular cell or a range of cells. You must go to the Home Tab Editing Find and Select Go To special to access it.

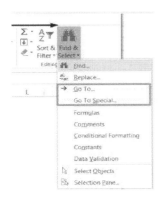

As you can see, it includes a variety of choices for selecting and using various types of cells.

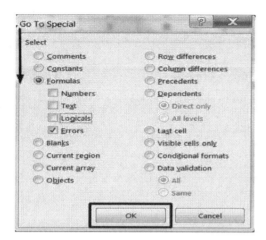

For example, if you want to pick all the blank cells, choose the blank and click OK, and all the blank cells will be selected quickly.

Similarly, suppose you wish to select cells with formulae and return numbers. In that case, you must first pick formulas, checkmark numbers, and click OK.

The Pivot Table

One of the most effective data evaluation methods is pivot tables. A summary table may be made from a huge data source. Follow the instructions below to create a pivot table:

To begin, go to the Insert Tab and choose the pivot table option.

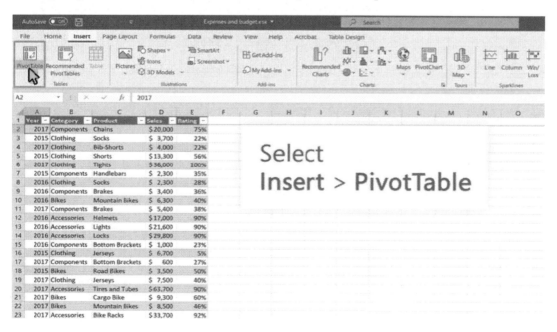

You'll be presented with a dialogue box where you may choose the source data, but since you've already picked the data, the range will be taken automatically.

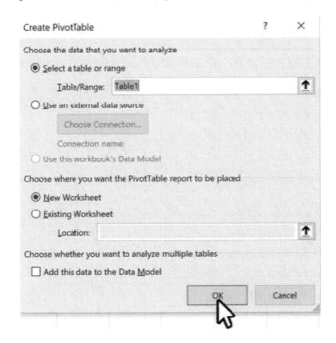

After you click OK, you'll see a sidebar similar to the one below, where you can drag and drop the rows, columns, and values for the pivot table. Now add Year, Category, Product, and Sales to the values to complete the table.

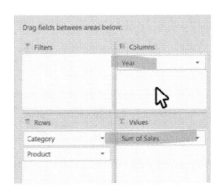

After defining everything, you'll get a pivot chart similar to the one below.

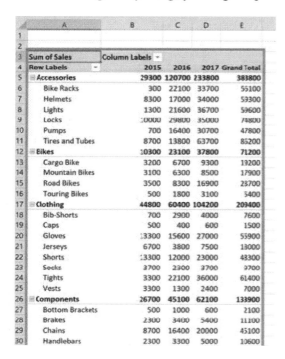

Sum of Sales	Column Labels			
Row Labels	2015	2016	2017	Grand Total
Accessories	29300	120700	233800	383800
Bike Racks	300	22100	33700	56100
Helmets	8300	17000	34000	59300
Lights	1300	21600	36700	59600
Locks	10000	29800	35000	74800
Pumps	700	16400	30700	47800
Tires and Tubes	8700	13800	63700	86200
Bikes	10300	23100	37800	71200
Cargo Bike	3200	6700	9300	19200
Mountain Bikes	3100	6300	8500	17900
Road Bikes	3500	8300	16900	28700
Touring Bikes	500	1800	3100	5400
Clothing	44800	60400	104200	209400
Bib-Shorts	700	2900	4000	7600
Caps	500	400	600	1500
Gloves	13300	15600	27000	55900
Jerseys	6700	3800	7500	18000
Shorts	13300	12000	23000	48300
Socks	3700	2300	3700	9700
Tights	3300	22100	36000	61400
Vests	3300	1300	2400	7000
Components	26700	45100	62100	133900
Bottom Brackets	500	1000	600	2100
Brakes	2300	3400	5400	11100
Chains	8700	16400	20000	45100
Handlebars	2300	3300	5000	10600

Named range

Giving a cell or a range of cells a name is known as a named range. Every cell in Excel has a unique address that combines row and column.

However, with the named range, you may assign that cell or that range of cells a particular name (Generic) and then refer to it by that name.

Imagine you have a tax percentage in cell A1; instead of utilizing the reference, you can now assign it a name and utilize it in all calculations.

Go to the Formula Tab and choose Define Names. Define a name to create a named range.

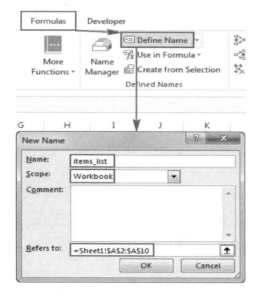

- The range's name.

- You can use that range across the workbook or only in the worksheet.

- If you have any to add, please do so in the comments.

- Then there's the cell's or range's address.

After you click OK, Excel will give that name to cell A1, and you may use it in calculations to refer to it.

You may establish a named range for the range of cells in the same manner and then refer to it in formulae.

Conditional Formatting

The fundamental concept of conditional formatting is to apply to format using conditions and formulae, and the most significant part is that there are more than 20 possibilities available with a single click.

For example, if you want to highlight all duplicate values in a range of cells, you must go to the Home Tab and choose Conditional Formatting Highlight Rules Duplicate Values.

In addition, you may use data bars, color talents, and icons.

Using Sparklines

Sparklines are little charts that may be inserted into a cell and based on a data set. To add a sparkline, go to the Insert Tab and choose Sparklines.

	A	B	C	D	E	F	G
1	Jan	Feb	Mar	Apr	May	June	
2	45	66	57	84	64	51	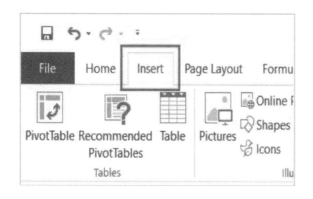
3	45	66	57	84	64	51	
4	1	1	-1	1	-1	-1	

You may use three different sorts of sparklines in a cell.

Line

Column

Win-Loss

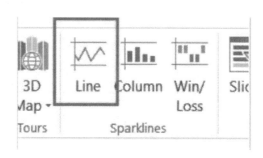

When you click the dazzling button, a dialogue box asks you to pick the data range and the sparkling's destination range.

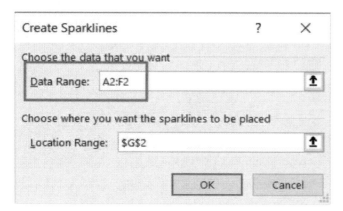

Aside from that, the sparkline tab allows you to personalize a sparkline by altering its color, adding markings, and more.

The Tool for Quick Analysis

As its name implies, the Quick Analysis Tool enables you to evaluate data with only one or two clicks. It offers certain pre-selected choices that may assist you in analyzing and presenting data. When you choose a student's data with their score, a little icon appears at the bottom of the screen, the button for the rapid analysis tool.

When you click on it, a few tabs appear, from which you may choose alternatives. Let's take a look at each tab individually now.

Formatting: This tab lets you apply conditional formatting to the chosen table, such as data bars, color scales, icon sets, and other rules.

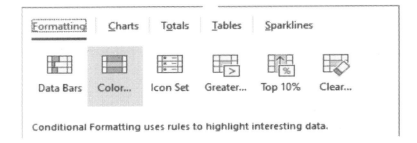

Charts: This page displays some of the suggested charts that you may use with the data you've chosen, or you can click on more charts to choose a particular chart.

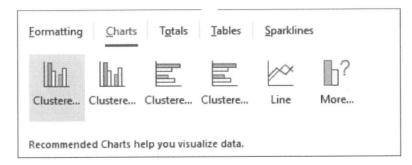

Total: You can rapidly add some of the fundamental calculations, such as average count, running total, and many more, from this page.

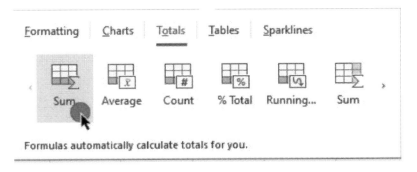

Table: You may insert a pivot table with the specified data and apply an Excel table from this tab.

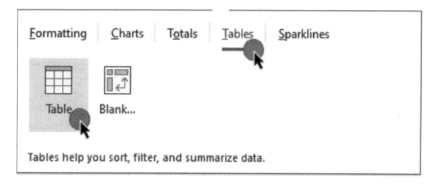

Sparklines: You may use this tab to add sparklines, which are little charts you can make inside a cell.

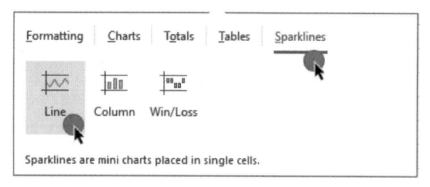

Keyboard Shortcuts to Know

Before you begin, keep in mind that while the list is lengthy, it is in no way comprehensive. However, we've compiled a list of the most helpful shortcuts and hope you'll find them useful.

- Press Ctrl + N: To make a fresh workbook

- Press Ctrl + S: To save a workbook

- Press Ctrl + O: To access a saved workbook

- Press Ctrl + A: To pick all of the contents of a workbook

- Press Ctrl + C: To copy highlighted cells.

- Press Ctrl + B: To make highlighted cells bold

- Press Ctrl + D: To copy the contents of the cell above into the chosen cell.

- Press Ctrl + F: To look for something in a workbook

- Press Ctrl + H: To locate and replace cell contents

- Press Ctrl + G: To jump to a certain location with a single button

- Press Ctrl + I: To italicize cell contents

- Press Ctrl + L: To open the build table dialogue box

- Press Ctrl + K: To insert a hyperlink in a cell

- Press Ctrl + P: To print a workbook

- Press Ctrl + U: To underline highlighted cells

- Press Ctrl + R to copy the cell's contents on the left into the chosen cell.

- Press Ctrl + V: To paste everything that was saved

- Press Ctrl + Z: To reverse the previous operation

- Press Ctrl + W: To close your new workbook

- Press Ctrl + 1: To format the contents of a cell

- Press Ctrl + 8: To display the outline symbols

- Press Ctrl + 5: To place a strikethrough in the cell

- Press Ctrl + 9: To hide a row

- Press Ctrl + 0: For hide a column

- Press Ctrl +Shift +: To enter the present time in a cell

- Press Ctrl +. : For the move from showing cell values to formulas

- Press Ctrl + ; : To insert the date in a cell

- Press Ctrl + ': To copy the formula from the cell above

- Press Ctrl +Shift + = : For insert rows and columns

- Press Ctrl+ - : For erase columns or rows

- Press Ctrl +Shift + : For differentiate between formulas & their values in cells,

- Press Ctrl +Shift +!: To apply comma formatting

- Press Ctrl +Shift + @ : For apply time formatting

- Press Ctrl +Shift + $: For apply currency formatting,

- Press Ctrl +Shift + percent: To apply percentage formatting

- Press Ctrl +Shift + # : For apply date formatting

- Press Ctrl +Shift + & : For position borders around the selected cells

- Press Ctrl + - : For erase a selected row or column

- Press Ctrl +Shift + : For delete a border

- Press Ctrl + Spacebar: To pick an entire column

- Press Ctrl + Home: To return to cell A1

- Press Ctrl +Shift + Spacebar: To pick an entire workbook

- Press Ctrl +Shift + Tab: To return to the previous workbook

- Press Ctrl +Shift + O: To pick the cells containing statements

- Press Ctrl +Shift + F: To open the fonts menu under format cells

- Press Ctrl +Drag: To repeat a worksheet or drag and transfer a cell

- Press Ctrl +Shift + Drag : For insert a copy

- Press Ctrl +Up arrow: To go to the top most cell in the current column

- Press Ctrl +Right arrow: To go to the last cell in the selected row

- Press Ctrl +Down arrow: To move to the last cell in the current column

- Press Ctrl +Left arrow: To return to the 1st cell in the selected row

- Press Alt +Page down: To move the screen to the right

- Press Ctrl +End: To go to the last cell in a workbook

- Press Alt Page Up: To move the screen to the left

- Press Ctrl + F1: To expand or compress the Ribbon

- Press Ctrl +F2: For the open print preview pane

- Press Alt: To open the control keys

- Press Alt +F +T: To use the options

- Press the tab key: To toggle to the next cell

- Press Alt +Down arrow: To activate cell filters,

- Press F3: If cells have been named, paste a cell name

- Press F2: To edit a cell

- Press Shift + F2: To add or edit the cell comment

- Press Alt +H +B: To add a border

- Press Alt + H +H: To choose a fill color

- Press Ctrl + 9: To hide selected rows

- Press Esc Enter: To cancel the entry

- Press Ctrl + 0 : For hide selected columns

- Press Shift +Left arrow: To extend the cell range to the left

- Press Shift +Right arrow: To extend the cell range to right

- Press Shift +Space: To select the entire row

- Press Alt + H: To get to the Home tab in the Ribbon

- Press Alt + P: To open the Page Layout tab in the Ribbon

- Press Alt + N: To open the Insert tab in the Ribbon

- Press Alt + M: To open the Formulas tab in the Ribbon

- Press Alt + R: To open the Review tab in the Ribbon

- Press Alt + A: To open the Data tab in the Ribbon

- Press Alt + W: To open the View tab in the Ribbon

- Press Alt + Y: To open the Help tab in the Ribbon

- Press Alt + Q: To quickly jump to the search

- Press Shift + F3: To open the Insert feature dialogue window

- Press Alt +Enter: To start a new line in the current cell

- Press F9: For calculate workbooks

- Press Ctrl +Alt + F9: To force all workbooks to be calculated

- Press Shift + F9: To calculate an active worksheet

- Press Ctrl + F3: For open name manager

- Press Ctrl +Alt + + : For zoom in on a workbook

- Press Ctrl + Shift +F3: To build names from values in columns and rows

- Press Ctrl +Alt +: To zoom out inside the workbook

- Press Alt +2: To save a workbook

- Press Alt +1: To enable Autosave

- Press Alt +F + Z: To share your workbook

- Press Alt +F + E: To export your workbook

- Press Alt or F11: To switch key tips on or off

- Press Alt +F + C: To close & save your workbook

- Press Alt +Y + W: To see what's fresh in Microsoft Excel

- Press Ctrl + F4: To close Microsoft Excel

- Press F1: For open Microsoft Excel support

Excel Tricks

1. Color Customization of your tabs.

When you have a lot of separate sheets in one workbook — which happens to most of us — color-code the tabs to make things easy to find where you need to go. You may, for example, color code last month's marketing records red and this month's green.

To change the color of a page, simply right-click it and choose "Tab Color." A popup would appear, allowing you to choose a color from an established theme or customize one to suit your requirements.

2. Adding a comment in a cell.

When you like to make a note or apply a comment to a particular cell in a worksheet, right-click your desired cell and select Insert Comment from the list. To save your message, type it into the text box and then press outside your comment box.

A small red triangle appears in the corner of cells that hold comments. Click over the comment to see it.

3. Copy & duplicate formatting.

If you've spent hours editing a sheet to your preference, you'll admit it's not the most pleasurable experience. On the contrary, it's

As a result, you're unlikely to choose to — or need to — replicate the procedure the next time. Instead, you can conveniently copy

Pick what you wish to duplicate, then go to the dashboard and select the Format Painter choice (the paintbrush icon). As seen below, the pointer can turn into a paintbrush, allowing you to pick the cell, document, or whole worksheet to that you want to add the formatting.

4. Identify duplicate values.

Duplicate values, including duplicate content regarding SEO, may be problematic if left unchecked in some instances. However, in certain situations, what you need to do is be mindful of it.

Whatever the case, it's simple to find current duplicate values in your worksheet by following a few simple measures. To do so, pick Highlight Cell Rules >Duplicate Values from the Conditional Formatting menu.

Build a formatting rule to determine which kind of repeated content you want to bring forward using the popup.

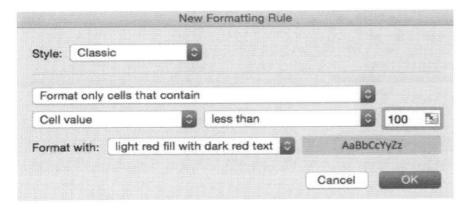

Formatted duplicate cells in yellow in the illustration above to distinguish any duplicate salaries within the chosen range.

Chapter 7: How Advanced Users can Use Excel

Whether you want to create professional-looking reports or just need to learn more about Excel for advanced users, this course will provide you with the necessary information. In this course, you will learn the most current data visualization and manipulation tools and best practices for using these tools. You'll also complete interactive exercises to master the basics of the program. The results will be as impressive as your work. You'll feel confident tackling any project that requires advanced Excel skills.

Complex Formulas and Functions

There are many cool features to learn regarding advanced excel formulas and functions. For example, you can use conditional formatting in Excel to select different outputs based on certain conditions. You can also use this formula to chop text strings into chunks that you can paste into charts. You'll soon understand how useful these features can be in managing errors.

The LEFT function pulls part of the data from the left of the cell. The RIGHT function does the same thing but allows you to independently set the value of the left column. In addition, you can combine multiple values from different columns with the RIGHT function. You can also use the LEFT and RIGHT functions in one formula if you need to simultaneously manipulate the values of several columns. By learning to use both types of advanced Excel formulas and functions, you'll be on your way to creating complex spreadsheets.

VLOOKUP

The VLOOKUP function in MS Excel allows you to look up specific information about a particular item. For example, this feature will enable you to enter the details of a particular item, such as a specific grade, and find out if that grade has already been assigned to another item. VLOOKUP can also look up a single item from an inventory list. The following steps will guide you through the process. If you are unfamiliar with VLOOKUP, you can use a short video to get an overview.

First, identify the column you'd like to fill in. Next, select the Functions tab and choose VLOOKUP. You can then type the formula into the highlighted cell. In addition, you can type the lookup value and column number into the formula. Once you've done this, click the "Done" button. This will populate the first cell. You can also check the value of your VLOOKUP formula by clicking the tiny square on the bottom right corner of the cell.

When using VLOOKUP, you should be careful with your input value. The lookup value can be a number or a text string. If it's a number, you don't need to use quotes; the default value is TRUE. The range_lookup parameter specifies whether the lookup value must be exact or approximate. If it's not, you can specify an approximate match.

| | E2 | | f_x | =VLOOKUP(E1, A2:B7, 2, FALSE) | | |

	A	B	C	D	E	F
1	**Animal**	**Speed(mph)**		**Animal**	Antelope	
2	Cheetah	70		**Speed**	61	
3	Zebra	59				
4	Antelope	61				
5	Lion	50				
6	Elk	45				
7	Coyote	43				
8						

SUMIF

There are several ways to use SUMIF in Excel. This function sums values based on the condition they match. It can also be used to sum values in a different column. To use this function, you must know how to input a condition and a cell range. Then, you can use wildcard operations or a single character to match the condition. However, SUMIF is not a good choice when you have multiple conditions.

To use SUMIF with a date range, you must supply it in the correct format for Excel. The DATE function can help you determine which date formats are supported. You can also use a date range or multiple criteria to create the desired calculation. The dates are entered in the A and B columns in the example below. To determine the total number of units sold, enter the total amount for each month in column B.

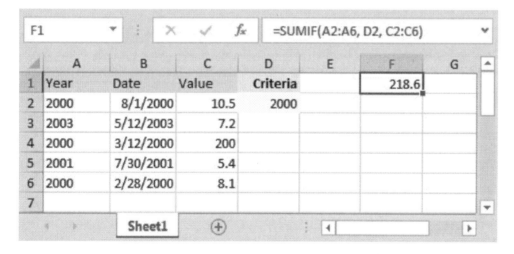

| | F1 | | | f_x | =SUMIF(A2:A6, D2, C2:C6) | | |

	A	B	C	D	E	F	G
1	Year	Date	Value	Criteria		218.6	
2	2000	8/1/2000	10.5	2000			
3	2003	5/12/2003	7.2				
4	2000	3/12/2000	200				
5	2001	7/30/2001	5.4				
6	2000	2/28/2000	8.1				
7							

Sheet1

Example

To display named ranges, go to the top of the screen's toolbar and pick the Formulas tab. Select Name Manager from the Defined Names drop-down menu in the Defined Names group.

The Name Manager's window should now appear.

RUNDOWN

The ROUNDDOWN function returns a value rounded down to a given number of values.

The ROUNDDOWN function is a Number Function that is built-in in Excel.

The syntax is: ROUNDDOWN (number, digits)

Example:

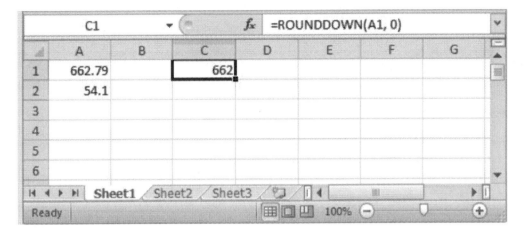

ROUNDDOWN (A1, 0)

Result is 662

ROUNDUP

In Microsoft Excel, the ROUNDUP function generates a number that rounds up to a specified number of values.

The ROUNDUP function in Excel is a built-in function classified as a number function.

The syntax is ROUNDUP(number, digits)

Example:

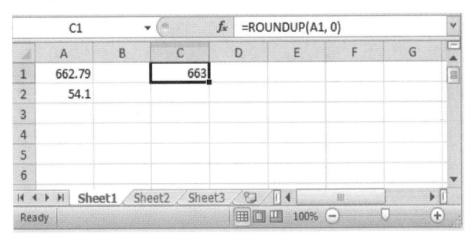

ROUNDUP(A1, 0) Result is 663

TEXT

The TEXT function produces a result converted to text in a specific format. The TEXT function is a Text Function built-in function in Excel. For example, in a worksheet cell, the TEXT function may be utilized as a part of a formula.

The syntax is TEXT (value, format)

Example:

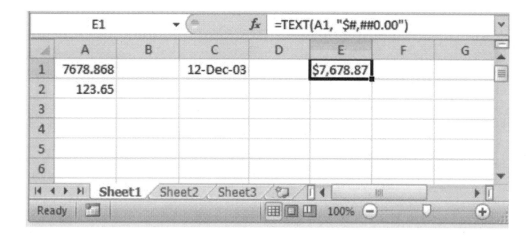

Based on the Excel file above, the following TEXT samples would be returned:

=TEXT(A1, "$#,##0.00")

The final figure is $7,678.87.

AND

The AND function in Microsoft Excel returns TRUE if all criteria are true. It returns FALSE if any of the criteria are false. The AND function is a logical function that is incorporated into Excel.

Syntax is AND (condition1, [condition2], ...)

Example:

	A	B	C	D	E	F
	E2	f_x =AND(C1>10, D1>40)				
1	**Raw Data**	**TRIM**				
2	China 2022	China 2022	50	48	FALSE	
3	2021 India	2021 India	700	5		
4	United States 2022	United States 2022	48	6		
5	Indonesia 2021	Indonesia 2021	89	7		
6	Pakistan 2023	Pakistan 2023	29	8		
7	Nigeria 2025	Nigeria 2025	53	3		
8	Brazil 2021	Brazil 2021	762	9		
9	Bangladesh 2020	Bangladesh 2020	533	6		
10	Russia 2019	Russia 2019	43	2		
11	Mexico 2018	Mexico 2018	267	4		
12						

Based on the Excel spreadsheet above, the following AND samples would be returned:

=AND(A1>10, A1>40)   The result is FALSE.

IF

The IF function in Microsoft Excel delivers one value if the condition is TRUE and another value if the condition is FALSE. The IF function is a Logical Function that is built-in in Excel.

Syntax is IF(condition, value if true, [value if false])

Example:

	A	B	C	D	E
	E6	f_x =IF(C6>10, "Reorder", "")			
1	**Raw Data**	**TRIM**			
2	China 2022	China 2022	50	48	FALSE
3	2021 India	2021 India	700	5	
4	United States 2022	United States 2022	48	6	
5	Indonesia 2021	Indonesia 2021	89	7	
6	Pakistan 2023	Pakistan 2023	29	8	Reorder
7	Nigeria 2025	Nigeria 2025	53	3	
8	Brazil 2021	Brazil 2021	762	9	
9	Bangladesh 2020	Bangladesh 2020	533	6	
10	Russia 2019	Russia 2019	43	2	
11	Mexico 2018	Mexico 2018	267	4	

=IF(c6>10, "Reorder", "")   "Reorder" is the outcome.

91

COUNT

The COUNT function is used to determine the number of cells in a range that contain numerical information. The COUNT function is a Statistical/Counting Function built-in in Excel.

Syntax is COUNT [argument2,... argument n])

Example:

	A	B	C	D	E	F
		fx =COUNT(D2:D11)				
1	Raw Data	TRIM				
2	China 2022	China 2022	50	48		
3	2021 India	2021 India	700	5		10
4	United States 2022	United States 2022	48	6		
5	Indonesia 2021	Indonesia 2021	89	7		
6	Pakistan 2023	Pakistan 2023	29	8		
7	Nigeria 2025	Nigeria 2025	53	3		
8	Brazil 2021	Brazil 2021	762	9		
9	Bangladesh 2020	Bangladesh 2020	533	6		
10	Russia 2019	Russia 2019	43	2		
11	Mexico 2018	Mexico 2018	267	4		
12						
13						
14						
15						
16						

=COUNT (d2:d11).   The final result is 10.

IF combined with AND/OR

Syntax:

=IF(AND(C4>=C2,C2<=C5),C7,C6)

models understand how difficult nested IF formulas can be. Combining the IF function with the AND or OR function may

Make calculations simpler to audit and comprehend for other users. The example below shows how we combined the separate functions to create a more complicated formula.

	A	B	C	D	E	F	G
1							
2		Data Cell	150				
3							
4		Condition 1	100	>=			
5		Condition 2	999	<=			
6		Result if true	100				
7		Result if fales	0				
8							
9		Live Formula	=IF(AND(C2>=C4,C2<=C5),C6,C7)				
10							
11							

Functions of CELL, LEFT, MID, and RIGHT

These sophisticated Excel functions may generate some complicated and advanced formulae. For example, the CELL function may return various data about a cell's contents (such as its name, location, row, column, and more). The LEFT method returns the text from the cell's beginning (left to right), the MID function delivers text from any cell's start point (left to right), and the RIGHT function returns the text from the cell's finish (right to the left).

PMT and IPMT

You'll need to know these two formulae if you work in commercial banking, real estate, FP&A, or any other financial analyst role that works with debt schedules.

The PMT formula calculates the value of making equal payments throughout a loan's life. You may use it in combination with IPMT (which shows you how much interest you'll pay on the same loan) and then separate principal and interest payments.

Here's how to use the PMT formula to calculate the monthly mortgage payment for a $1 million loan with a 5% interest rate over 30 years.

Syntax is =PMT(interest rate, # of periods, present value)

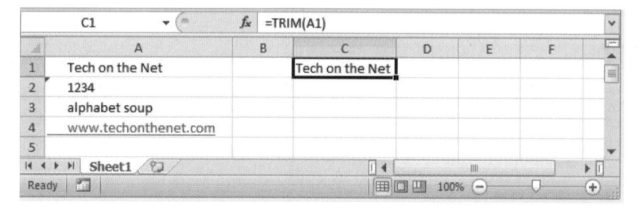

	A	B	C	D	E
1					
2					
3		Rate	5.0%		
4		# Periods	30		
5		Loan Value	1,000,000		
6					
7		PMT	=-PMT(C3,C4,C5,,1)	Formula	
8		PMT	61,954	Value	
9		Monthly PMT	5,163		
10					

TRIM

The TRIM function in MS Excel returns a text value that has the leading and following spaces removed. It is used to reduce unwanted spaces between words in a string. The TRIM function is an Excel built-in function classified as a Text Function.

Syntax: TRIM (text)

Example:

C1	▼	f_x	=TRIM(A1)

	A	B	C	D	E	F
1	Tech on the Net		Tech on the Net			
2	1234					
3	alphabet soup					
4	www.techonthenet.com					
5						

Sheet1

Ready   100%

=TRIM (A1) Result is "Tech on the Net."

LEN

The LEN function in MS Excel returns the length of the provided string. The LEN function is an Excel built-in function classified as a String/Text Function. Therefore, Excel can use it as a worksheet equation (WS) and a VBA formula (VBA).

Syntax: LEN (text)

A string's length can be determined using the Len function in Excel, defined as the total number of characters in the string. LEN is the same as syntax (text)

Please keep in mind that gaps are taken into consideration while determining length. (A1) gives 18

B1		X ✓ fx	=LEN(A1)	
	A	B	C	D
1	Learn Excel Easily	18		
2				
3				
4				
5				
6				

Upload data from websites

Advanced users of Excel can use the online spreadsheet application to upload data to their worksheets. The file format for an Excel spreadsheet is XLSX. Excel can import these files from a website, URL, or local file. For importing XLSX files, you need to use an ODBC driver. Excel can also accept real-time data through various programming interfaces. The application can also communicate with websites like Bloomberg and Reuters through add-ins like Power Plus Pro.

Chapter 8: Tables in Microsoft Excel

If you're wondering what a table is, this article will explain what a table is in Microsoft Excel and how to create one. I'll also list some of the advantages of using an Excel table. So read on to learn more! The benefits of using an Excel table are numerous. Below is a brief list of the most common uses for these tables. You can also see a list of some of the characteristics of a good table.

An overview of Excel tables

If you've ever used Excel, you know that tables are a great way to organize information. These can help you view trends and compare data from different sources. The process for creating an Excel table is quite straightforward. First, choose the data you want to organize in a table. Click Next to continue. Next, select a table format from the menu. If you don't want your data to appear in a table, click No.

A table is a dynamic grouping of cells, often with automatic updates and data aggregation. The table format allows users to visually group cells related by name. When a table is created, the formatting is automatically updated as the data changes. This makes it easy to find specific data and analyze the results quickly. As you work with data, tables evolve and grow. The formulas in these tables are also easier to read because they don't have to be copied to the next cell.

Structured references are another way to refer to data in an Excel table. Instead of using direct cell addresses in a formula, structured references allow you to reference a table by its name instead. You can use this feature in Excel formulas to reference tables inside the same workbook. To retrieve data from an external workbook, it is recommended to use references to cell ranges. The benefits of structured references are numerous. One of the most important is the ease with which you can create and use spreadsheets.

A table in Excel has built-in functions for data analysis and filtering. By default, the list of tables is blue and contains filters. When you save a table, you can name it will appear in the list. Using this method, you'll see a table called Table1, Table2, Table3, etc. This isn't very helpful for identifying a special table. Nevertheless, excel tables are a great way to organize data.

One of the essential functions of an Excel table is to display data. Therefore, the rows in the table should be named in a way that makes them easily readable. In Excel, columns in a table have unique headers, and names are placed in the top row. Moreover, you can customize the table's name using a "table name" box. Alternatively, you can change the name by clicking the Design tab in the properties group.

Create an Excel Table

You are ready to create the formatted Table after you have organized the data as mentioned above.

- Select a cell from the data list you prepared.
- Click the Insert tab from the Ribbon.
- Select the Table command from the Tables group.

- The range for your data should appear automatically in the Create Table dialogue box, and the My table has headers option should be checked. You can change the range and check the box if necessary.
- To accept these settings, click OK.

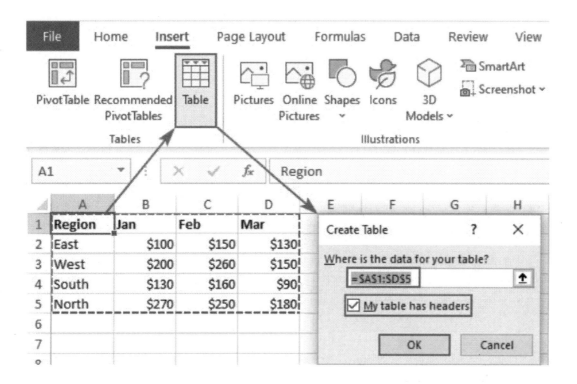

How to create a table in Microsoft Excel

When users add linked data to a spreadsheet, they may refer to such data as a "table," which is inaccurate terminology. To transform a range of cells into a table, you must first specify the format of the range of cells as a table. Therefore, finding more than one approach to do the same task in Excel is common.

Regardless of the approach you choose, Microsoft Excel will automatically pick the full block of cells in question. You then double-check that the range you've chosen is right, check or uncheck the option "My table includes headers," and click OK.

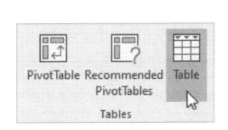

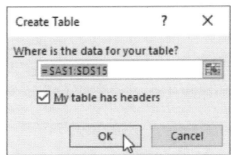

An attractively structured table is formed in your worksheet due to this. At first glance, it seems to be a standard range, complete with filter buttons in the header row, but there is much more to it!

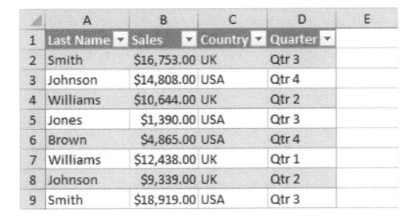

Advantages of using an Excel table

Using an Excel table has many advantages. It allows you to work faster since you can reference data as a group. For example, referencing data as a group makes it easier to write formulas and reduces the number of resources needed for calculations in Excel. A table allows you to quickly filter data, add totals, and build formulas in a shorter amount of time.

Tables make it easier to observe patterns and gain a clearer perspective on your data. However, the benefits of using an Excel table go far beyond enhancing your workflow.

One of the biggest benefits of an Excel table is that you can easily add more data to it. It makes adding data easier than ever before. You can add as many records as you need without worrying about formatting. There are many ways to add more data to an Excel table. Once you've set up your data, you can easily add formulas and data. You can also include summary calculations at the bottom of the data.

Another benefit of an Excel table is that it saves time. You don't have to scroll through columns and rows to select a cell. Instead, using shortcuts, you can make a connection between two cells or rows or duplicate one row. It also helps you identify patterns and improve your productivity.

Excel table characteristics

Excel tables include many useful features.

- **Has sorting and filtering integrated options**
- **Column heads remain visible even when scrolling down the page.**
- **Convenient formatting (Excel table styles)**
- **Automatic table growth to accommodate new information**

Chapter 9: Pivot Tables

You probably already know what a Pivot Table is, but are you sure you know how to use it? Read on to learn more about this useful tool. Pivot tables let you easily compare and contrast data. Its most useful feature is its ability to visualize data in different ways. Its flexibility is the most compelling reason to use it. You can even create your custom Pivot Tables. Fortunately, it's incredibly easy to create these tables!

What are Pivot Tables?

Pivot tables in MS Excel allow you to analyze your data in various ways. For example, you can use them to identify trends, compare data across categories, or make a report of the results of an analysis. This feature allows you to change the data without affecting the original export. Of course, you should always save your work before making changes to return to the previous version of the file later.

To create a pivot table, open a worksheet with the data you would like to analyze. Choose the New Worksheet option. Next, choose a location for the table in the worksheet. Click the Location box to select the first cell of data. Alternatively, select an existing worksheet. You can also select the Existing Worksheet option and place the pivot table on that worksheet. You can also choose to select a cell with data that already exists.

Pivot tables in MS Excel can summarize data from thousands of rows. Once you create a pivot table, you can choose to save it or reuse it in another Excel workbook. In the XLSX file, you can also reuse existing pivot tables. Be sure to rename them according to the date they were exported. By doing this, you can avoid wasting time creating multiple worksheets. If you need to change the layout of the pivot table, you can also choose to use the existing Excel file with the same data.

Why are Pivot Tables Important?

The basic idea behind Pivot Tables is to compare a single data table with multiple ones. Pivot Tables contain columns of data that are ordered based on their field names. You can easily compare Pivot Tables by dragging and dropping fields from one column to another. These fields will automatically update the Pivot Table in the worksheet. There are many options for report layout, including redundant ones.

The data in a pivot table is referred to as the Source Data. The data is either contained in the worksheet or sourced from an external database. Pivot Tables are useful when you want to summarize thousands of rows of data. You can drag and drop fields to populate the values. Then, when you need to change a field's value, just drag and drop the data into the corresponding field and click "update" or "refresh" to get the updated information.

Another benefit of pivot tables is that they are easy to create. They don't require complex formulas; you can set them up in minutes. That means less work and faster results. Organize the source data properly before starting the process of making pivot tables. A well-designed pivot table can help you avoid redundancies and make your analysis more accurate. And as you can see, there are many benefits to using them in your work with Excel.

Creating Pivot Tables

Pivot tables can be used to get all the data together while still allowing you to process and sort it in various ways. Tick the beside the field name to build a PivotTable, and right-click the field name to select a place to shift the object to (i.e., Add to Column Labels, Add to Row Labels, Add to Report Filter, and Add to Values).

Options for creating a Pivot Table

You may also move an object from the Pivot Table Category List to one of the fields below by clicking on each field name, keeping down the cursor, and moving it to one of the fields below.

The Pivot Table fields

The most exciting thing to note regarding Pivot Tables is that they allow you to generate relevant data without needing to pick and enter it manually. Often, keep in mind that any changes you create can be quickly undone if you later find they aren't essential.

A PivotTable Field List disappears when you click outside the layout region (of a PivotTable report). Click within the PivotTable layout region or report to restore the field list.

Class, as an example, you'll add a few of the required fields into columns and rows and use the Pivot Table you just created so you can start working with the results. First, in the Rows sector, type Topic, and in the Values field, type Ex. Teacher and Ex. Course.

Mostly on the left side of a report, the information in the Subject area is automatically shown as rows. The data in Ex. Course and Ex. The teacher, which does include figures, appears accurately in a right-hand field. It will immediately show us the number of these fields for every subject matter. Click the downward arrow in front of each value in the fields array, Values > >Value Field Settings >> Average, or right-clicking on the column title inside the PivotTable to adjust this to average. It's worth noting that you have many choices to choose from.

Click PivotTable Analyze Behavior >> Actions party >> Clear >> Clear Everything on the Ribbon to restart the report and delete all the fields so you can start again.

Sorting Data

Sort the data using different parameters, such as name, value, count, or other criteria, as the basic pivot table is in place. Next, click the auto-sort option and then "additional sort options" to select various criteria to sort the data. Another alternative is to right-click anywhere around the table and choose Sort, then "additional sort choices" from the menu.

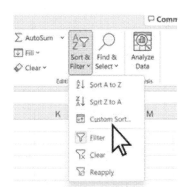

How to sort data

In MS Excel, sorting data rearranges the rows depending on the contents of a certain column. For example, sorting a table to place names in alphabetical order is a good idea. Alternatively, you might arrange data by amount from smallest to greatest or from biggest to smallest.

The steps for sorting a table are outlined below. First, choose the table, then select *Sort* and *Filter* from the Home menu. Next, a sorting dialogue box appears.

This dialogue box enables you to add more than one level of sorting to the usual one. For example, choose Column_name and A to Z in the Order box in the Sort by box.

In the sorting dialogue box, you may add a level of sorting. This would be beneficial for sorting tables such as those used in national population censuses.

Filtering Data

Adding a filter to the data is a simple method to sort it. With the filter feature, we may see data for particular sub-sections with a single click. An additional box appears at the top of the pivot table, indicating the filter has been applied by dragging the desired category from the list of choices down to the Filters section.

A filtering Filter is one of the most often used tools among Excel power users. It lets you pick what parts of a table you wish to see and conceal the rest.

It's simple to use and can be accessed from three distinct Excel locations. First, the filter may be accessed by right-clicking and choosing *Filter*. Next, select *Sort* and *Filter* from the Home menu on the right. From the Data dropdown menu. You'll notice a dropdown box beside the table headings after you've switched on the Filter tool by clicking on it. By selecting the dropdown box, you may see all the unique items in that area and choose which ones you wish to see (hiding the rest). All things are chosen by default, so you'll have to deselect the ones you don't want to view. Except for the BBQ Chicken, all the pizza toppings were left unselected in the screenshot below (meaning only BBQ Chicken was selected). The blue row numbers are Excel's method of graphically indicating that specific rows have been buried since they do not include the things we wish to look at.

Pivot tables are a terrific method to organize and analyze data in Microsoft Excel, and the more you know about them, the more you will get away with them. Filtering pivot table, for example, is a wonderful method to concentrate on certain data, and you'll frequently find this functionality included in dashboards. But Fortunately, a filtering pivot table is simple.

Before we can begin filtering, we will need a pivot table, so we'll create a pivot table shown in Figure A using the data from the same sheet. To do this, go to any point inside the data set and do the following steps:

Select *PivotTable* from the Tables group on the Insert tab.

Click *Existing Worksheet* options in the resulting dialogue to display the data and PivotTable simultaneously, and then enter the F1 (in Figure B) just as the location.

When you click *Ok*, Excel will show you a PivotTable frame and a field list.

Build a pivot table in Figure A using Figure C as a reference.

Figure A

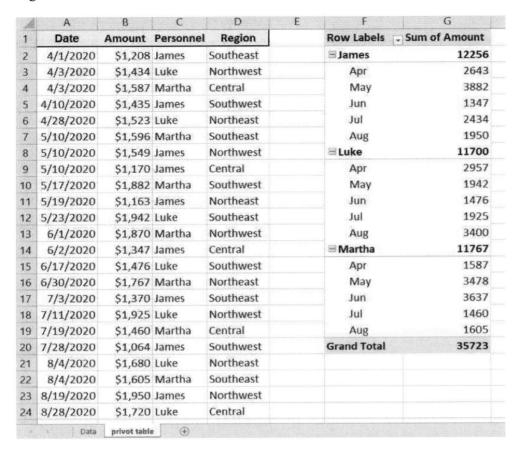

Figure B

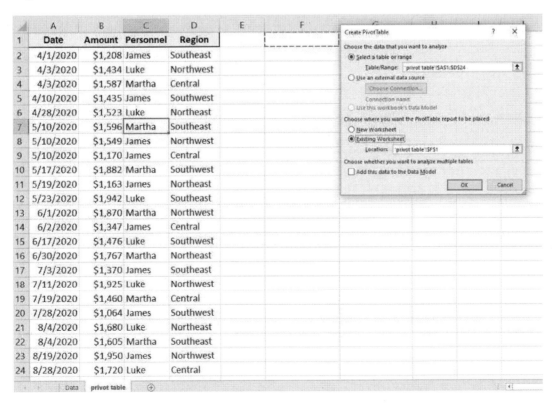

Figure C

This simpler pivot table shows the daily amount for each individual, aggregating amounts that fall on the same day. Since there is a date, Excel automatically inserts date components, like a quarter, month, and year. I've kept month as the default. The order of the data in data collection is unimportant. The PivotTable is a nice report in itself. However, you may want to concentrate on certain data.

Filtering is as simple as that.

Change Summary Calculation

By default, all data in Excel pivot tables are presented as the total of whatever is displayed in the table. Right-click on the data to alter the value and choose "Value field settings," which will open the box. It is a critical characteristic in accounting and financial analysis since switching between units/volume (the count function) and overall cost or income (the sum function) is often required.

Two-dimensional Pivot Table

A pivot table with fields on both rows and columns is a two-dimensional one.

Follow the steps outlined below to build two-dimensional pivot tables:

- Turn on the Datasheet.

- Select the INSERT tab.

- Select Pivot Chart & Table from the drop-down menu.

- Select all of the information.

- Choose the OK button

- With the pivot table tools, a new sheet will generate.

- Choose the fields you want to work with.

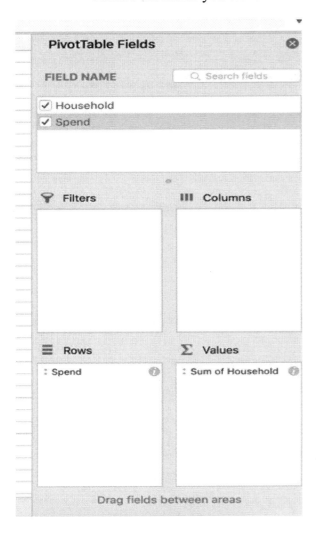

Different fields for Pivot tables

Chapter 10: Excel Charts

Excel is used to store data by firms of all sizes and in a range of industries. In addition, Excel can aid you in transforming your spreadsheet data into charts and graphs to obtain a clear view of your data and make intelligent business decisions.

A Basic Understanding of Excel Charts

A visual chart representation of data that includes columns and rows is presented visually. Charts are often used to evaluate large data sets to identify trends and patterns.

A chart is a way to show data in both columns and rows in an easy way to read. Charts are often used to look at trends and patterns in data sets. Then let's say you have been keeping track of sales figures in Excel for the last three years. It's easy to figure out which year had the most sales with charts. You can also make charts to show how well you met your goals and did well.

Types of Charts

There are many different chart types in Microsoft Excel:

- Column Charts.

- Pie Charts

- Bar Charts.

- Line Charts.

- Combo Charts.

- Scatter Charts.

Column Charts

It is common for a Column Chart to show the categories on the horizontal (type) axis and the values on the vertical (value) axis simultaneously. Add data in columns or rows to come up with a column chart. Do this to make the chart. Use this when you want to compare values across several different things. The values are ordered vertically.

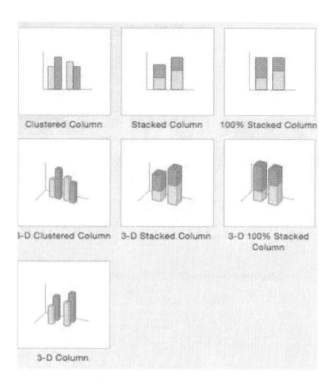

Pie Charts

We can plot a pie chart to represent data arranged in a column or row in a spreadsheet. Pie charts display element size for a data series in proportion to the total of the elements. The data points are shown as a percentage or portion of the whole pie chart.

This chart is recommended to be used when:

- Only a single data series exists.

- None of your data values is negative.

- Nearly none of your data values are zeros.

- You have less than seven groupings, all of them representing parts of the complete pie chart.

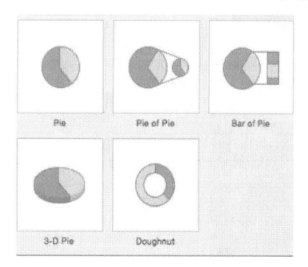

Bar Charts

The most significant distinction between a bar chart and a column chart is that the bars in a bar chart are horizontal rather than vertical in orientation. Even though both bar charts and column charts are often used, some people prefer column charts when dealing with negative values since it is easier to discern negatives when they are shown vertically on a y-axis.

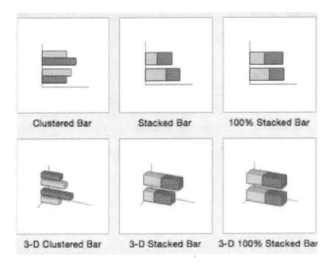

Line Charts

Line charts can show data that changes over time on an Axis of the same size. Because they show trends in data at regular intervals, such as months, quarters, or years, they are ideal for this type of thing. You can use line charts to show how things have changed, like months, days, or years.

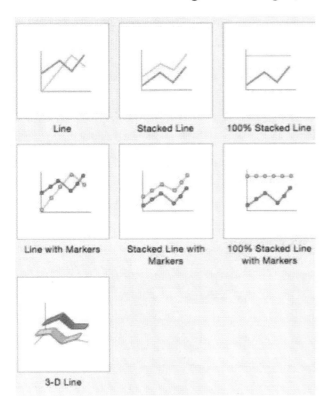

Combo Charts

The data is easier to understand when two or more chart types are used together, especially when the data is very different. It's shown with a second axis, making it easier to see and read. A Combo chart can be made by first putting the data in columns and rows on a spreadsheet. Then, you can use it when you want to show off different types of information simultaneously.

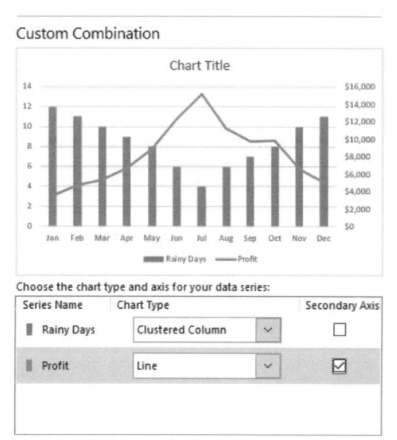

Bubble Charts

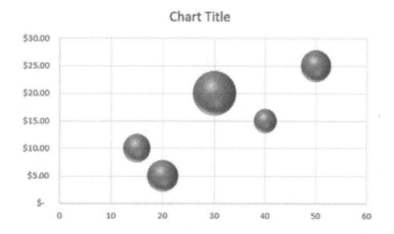

A Bubble graph appears similar to a Scatter graph but with an additional third column to clarify the scale of the bubbles that depict data points therein data sequence.

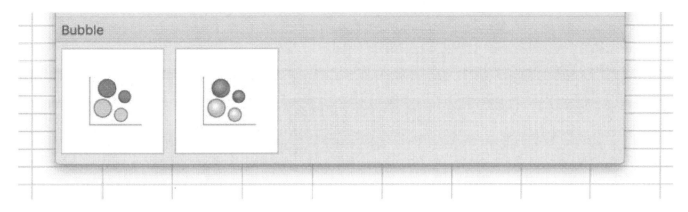

The subtypes of the Bubble Chart are as follows:

- Bubbles

- A three-dimensional visual effect bubble

- Stock Chart

As the name implies, stock style charts will show stock price changes. Nonetheless, the Stocks Chart may show changes in other figures, such as average rainfall or annual temperatures.

Place data into rows or columns in a specific order onto a worksheet to make a Stock graph. To make a simple low-high stock chart, e.g., arrange the data with Low-High- Close insert like Column Names in such an order. The subtypes of the Stocks Chart are as follows:

- High-low-proximity

- Amount of high-low-close

- Volume of Open-High-Close

- Open- closer-Higher-Lower

Scatter Charts

Scatter charts are used to display how one variable influences another. They are similar to line graphs in that they help display changes in variables over time. (This is referred to as correlation.) Bubble charts, a common chart type, are classified as scattered.

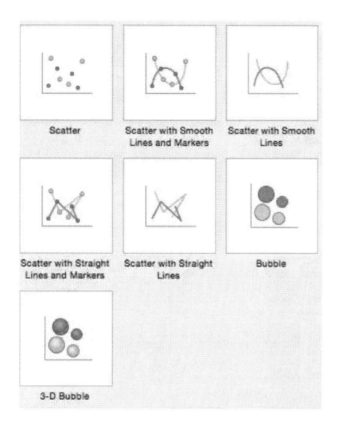

These are the seven scatter chart choices.

There are four additional chart categories. These charts are more case-specific:

- Area Charts.

- Stock Charts.

- Surface Charts.

- Radar Charts.

Area Charts

Area charts, like line charts, illustrate how values change over time. On the other hand, region charts are good for highlighting variances in change across several variables since the area beneath each line is solid.

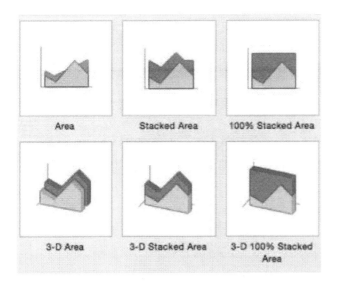

Stock Charts

Investors use this chart form to show a stock's low, high, and closing prices and financial analysis. However, if you choose to represent the range of a value (or the range of its expected value) and its exact value, you can use them in every case.

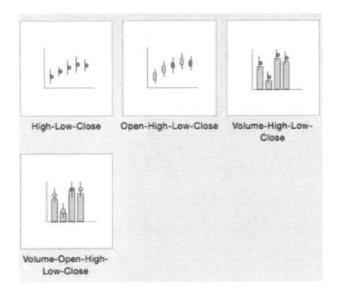

Surface Charts

To represent data over a 3-D landscape, use a surface chart. Big data sets, data sets of more than two variables, and data sets with groups inside a single variable benefit from the additional plane. Surface charts can be challenging to understand, so ensure the audience is comfortable with them.

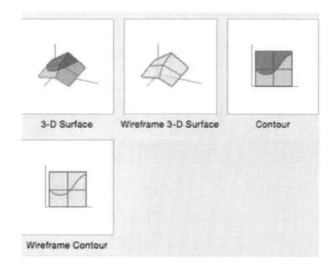

These are its types.

Radar Charts

A radar chart is useful for displaying data from different variables concerning one another. The central point is the starting point for all variables. The trick to using radar charts is to compare all particular factors concerning one another; they are often used to compare the weaknesses and strengths of various products or employees.

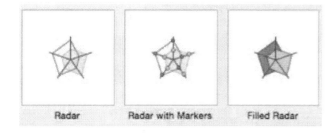

Radar Charts

Waterfall Chart Template for Excel

A waterfall chart template

These are the three kinds of radar charts.

Use of Different Excel Charts

Different Charts Have a Variety of Applications

The following are some examples of how various Excel charts might be used:

1. Column Chart:

Using column charts, you may compare data from comparable categories and see how the independence of variables changes over time. For example, compare and contrast the contributions of different class members and the differences between negative and positive values.

2. Bar Chart:

When the axis labels are too long to fit in a column chart, you may want to consider using a bar chart.

3. Pie Chart:

When you want to present a data composition that is 100 percent accurate, a pie chart is the best choice. To put it another way, a pie chart should only be used to depict the data composition when there is just one set of data and less than five categories to display on the chart. In general, pie charts represent the relationship between parts and the whole of your data. When your data is stated as a percentage, a pie chart is the most appropriate visual representation of your information. A pie chart should only be used when displaying data composition if the pie portions are the same size.

4. Scatter Chart:

A scatter chart is an excellent option when assessing and presenting the connection between two variables.

5. Line chart:

Line charts display and draw attention to data patterns, especially long-term trends between data values. Another situation in which a line chart may be appropriate is when you have many data points to present, and a column or bar chart would be too cluttered.

Charting Worksheet Data

Customizing and Formatting Elements of a chart

Adding chart components to a graph or chart above it by explaining details or adding meaning. You can choose a chart element (below the Home tab). You use the Add Chart Feature drop-down menu in the top-left corner

Choosing chart elements

To Hide or Display Axes

- Axes can be chosen. To view horizontal and vertical axes on your chart, Excel automatically pulls the column and row headers from your chosen cell set (Under Axes, there is a checkmark beside Primary Horizontal and Primary Vertical.)

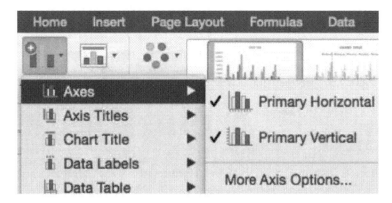

Displaying axes

- To delete the view axis from the chart, uncheck these choices. In this case, selecting Primary Horizontal deletes the year labels from your chart's horizontal axis.

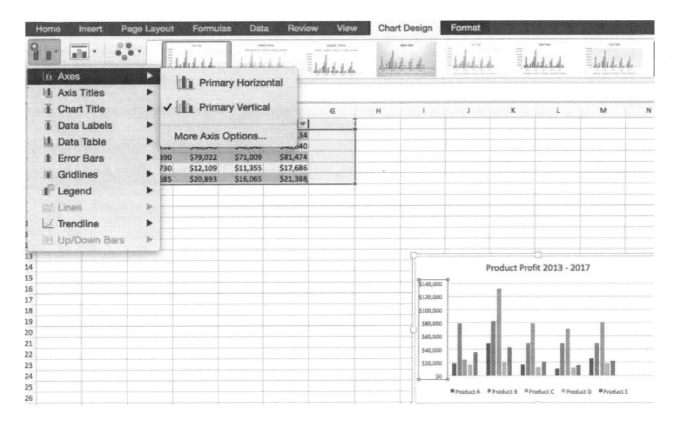

Hiding the axes

More Axis Choices opens a window with extra formatting and text options, such as inserting tick marks, identifiers, or numbers, or changing text color and height, from the Axes drop-down menu.

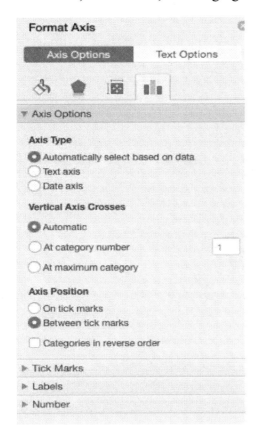

Extended choices on axes

To Add Axis Titles

Select Axis Title from the drop-down menu after clicking Add the Chart Element. Since axis names are not immediately added to charts in Excel, either the Primary Horizontal or Primary Vertical will be uncontrolled.

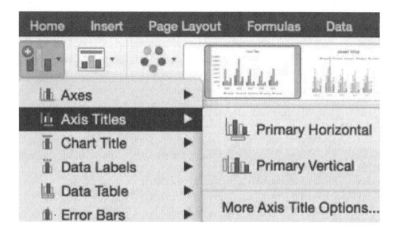

Adding a title to an axis

A script box will appear here on the chart when you press Primary Horizontal and Primary Vertical to generate axis names. In this case, press both. Fill in the axis titles. Add the titles "Year" and "Profit" to this example.

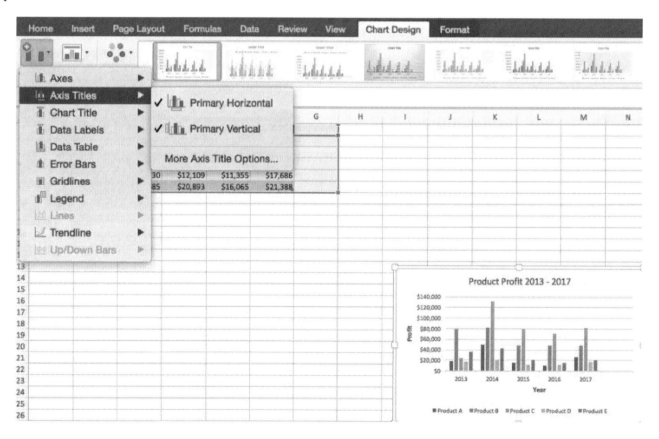

Naming the title

To Move or Remove Chart Title

Select Chart Title from the Add Chart Elements in the drop-down menu. The options available are None, Above the Chart, Focused Overlay, and Further Title Choices.

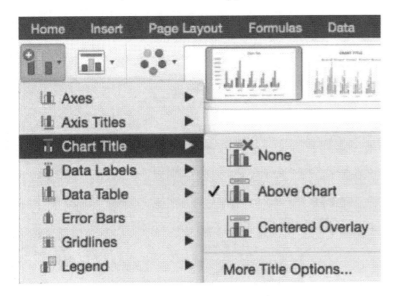

Moving or removing a chart title

To delete the chart title, choose None.

To put a title above your chart, click Above Chart. If you make one, Excel will automatically put a chart title above your chart.

To put the title inside the chart's gridlines, choose Centered Overlay. This alternative should be used cautiously: you wouldn't want your title to obscure data or clutter the graph (like in the example below).

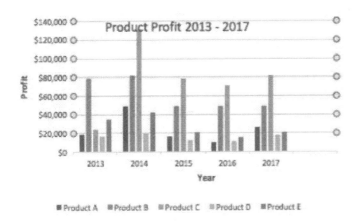

The centered overlay for a title

To Add Data Labels

Select Data Labels from the Add Chart Elements menu. There are six options for the data label titles: Middle, Inside End, Outside End, Inside Base, and More.

Adding data labels

Thanks to the four positioning choices, every data point calculated in your map have a unique mark. Select the desired option. This customization may be useful if you have a limited number of detailed data points or a lot of extra room in the chart. Adding data labels to the chart (clustered column), on the other hand, would certainly appear cluttered. This is how choosing the Center data label would appear, for instance.

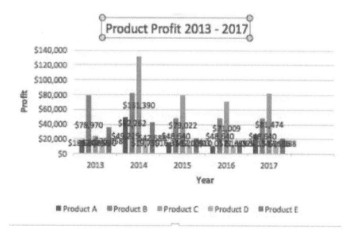

Centering the data label

To Add a Data Table

Select Data Table from the Add Chart Elements drop-down menu. By pressing Further Data Table Choices, you can use three pre-formatted options as well as an expanded menu:

Adding a data table

1. The default setting is None, meaning a data table isn't duplicated inside a chart.

2. Legend Keys shows the data set by displaying a table under the list. The legend is color-coded as well.

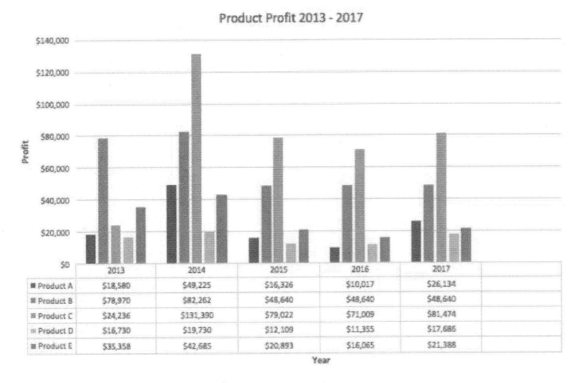

Product Profit 2013 - 2017

	2013	2014	2015	2016	2017
■ Product A	$18,580	$49,225	$16,326	$10,017	$26,134
■ Product B	$78,970	$82,262	$48,640	$48,640	$48,640
■ Product C	$24,236	$131,390	$79,022	$71,009	$81,474
■ Product D	$16,730	$19,730	$12,109	$11,355	$17,686
■ Product E	$35,358	$42,685	$20,893	$16,065	$21,388

■ Product A   ■ Product B   ■ Product C   ■ Product D   ■ Product E

The use of legend keys

3. A data table is often shown underneath the chart with No Legend Keys but without a legend.

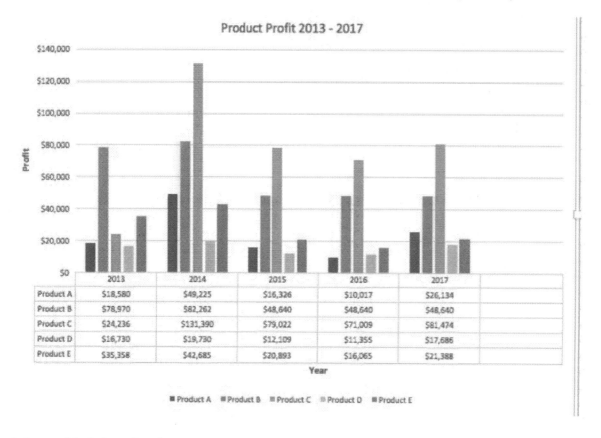

A data table below the chart

Note: If you plan to add a data table, you'll need to expand your chart to make room for it. To scale your chart, click on the corner and move it to the desired height.

To Add Error Bars

Select Error Bars from the Add Chart Elements menu. There are four choices on More Error Bar Options: None (default), 5% (Percentage), Standard Error, and Standard Deviation. Using various standard equations to isolate errors, error bars offer a visual image of a possible error in the displayed results.

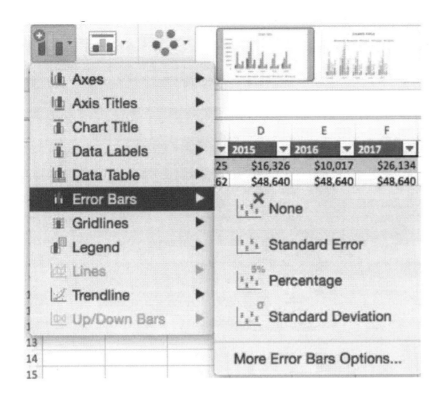

Adding error bars

When you choose Standard Error from the choices, you will see a chart like the one shown below.

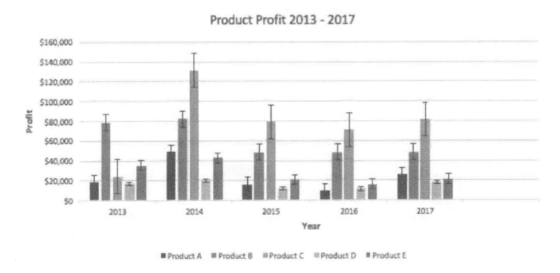

Displaying the standard error selection

To Add Gridlines

Gridlines can be added to a chart by clicking Add Chart Elements and then Gridlines. There are four variations: Prime Major Horizontal, Prime Major Vertical, Prime Minor Horizontal, and Prime Minor Vertical, whereas there are many Gridlines Options. For example, Excel automatically adds Prime Major Horizontal gridlines to a column table.

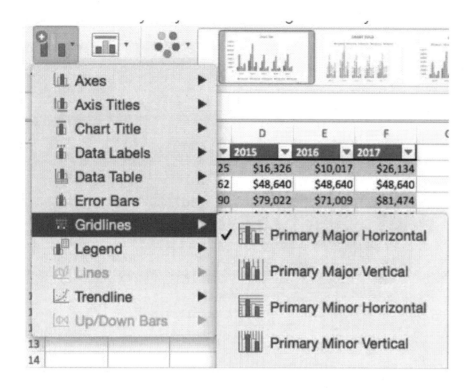

Adding gridlines

You can add as many distinct gridlines as possible by pressing all the options. For example, here's how your chart would appear with all four gridline choices selected:

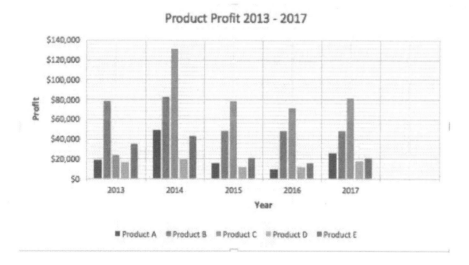

A chart with gridlines

To Add a Legend

Select Legend from the Add Chart Elements drop-down menu. There are five legend positioning options in contrast to the many Legend Preferences: None, Correct, Top, Left, and Bottom.

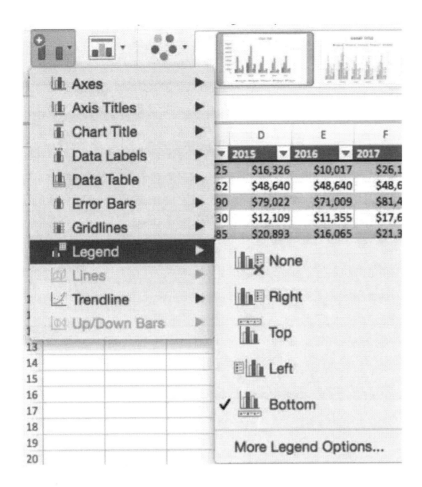

Adding a legend

The type and format of the chart will determine where the legend is placed. Select the option that appears to be the most appealing on your graph. When you choose the placement of the Right legend, this is what your chart looks like:

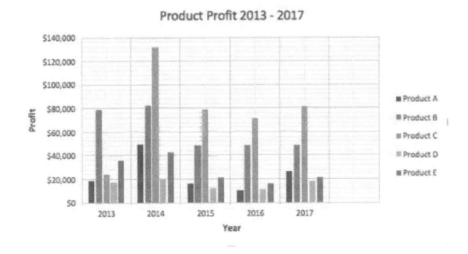

Legends displayed to the right of a chart

Adding Lines to a Clustered Column Chart: Lines aren't accessible for column charts (clustered). However, in some chart categories where you compare two factors, you can add lines to the chart after making the right choice (e.g., goal, average, comparison, etc.).

To Add a Trendline

Select Trendline from the Add Chart Elements drop-down menu. There are five choices: None (default), Linear Forecast, Linear, Exponential, and Moving Average, compared to Further Trendline Options. Again, be sure you're using the right tool for the data collection. In this case, you'll choose Linear.

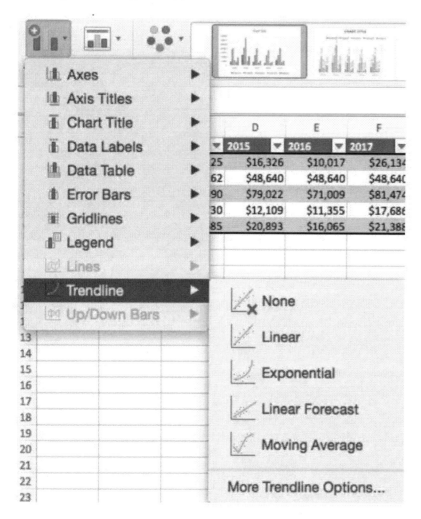

Adding trendlines

Excel provides the trendline for every commodity if you evaluate five different goods over time. Click on Product A and then the blue OK key to building the product's linear trendlines.

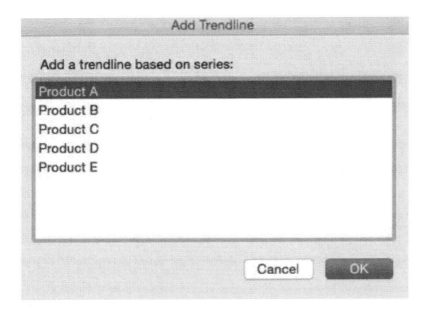

A trendline based on a specific series

The dotted trendlines will now appear on your chart to reflect the linear progression of Product A. The words "Linear (Product A)" have now been added to the legend.

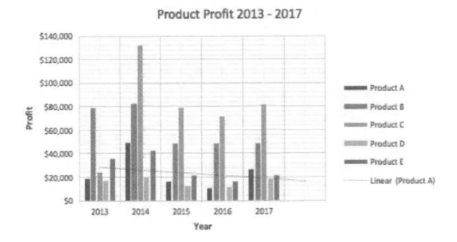

Trendline for Product A

Double-click on Trendlines to see a trendline equation in your chart. A Format Trendlines window will appear on the right-hand side of the screen. At the bottom of the window, check the box beside the Display equation in the chart. The equation is now visible on the chart.

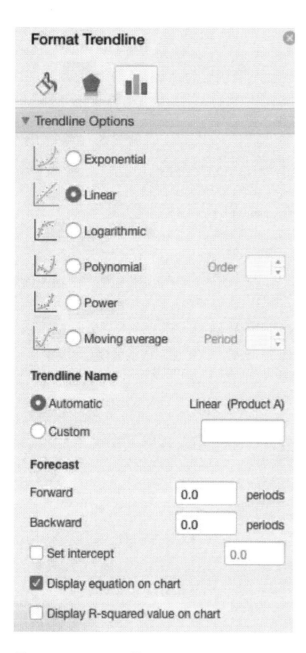

Formatting a trendline

Note: You can make as many trendlines as you like with each attribute in the chart. Here's an illustration of a chart of trendlines for Products A and C.

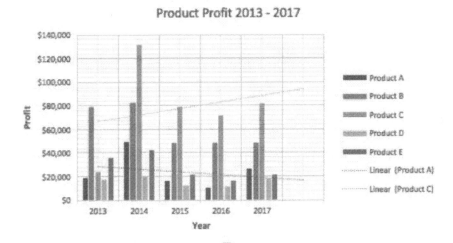

Trendline for products A and C

Up/Down Bars cannot be used in the column chart, yet they can be used in line charts to display rises and declines in data points.

Adjust a Quick Layout

Quick Layout is the toolbar's second drop-down menu, and it helps you easily adjust the layout of items in the chart (legends, titles, clusters, etc.).

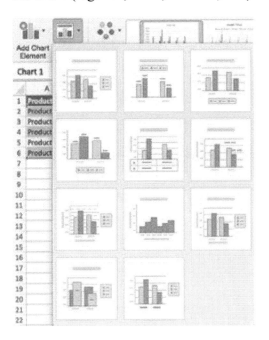

The Quick layout option

There are eleven quick layout choices. Hover the cursor over these various choices for a description, then choose what you need to use.

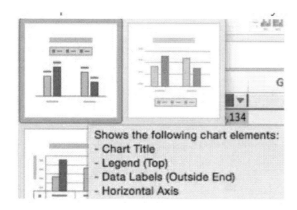

Shows the following chart elements:
- Chart Title
- Legend (Top)
- Data Labels (Outside End)
- Horizontal Axis

The quick layout choices

Change the Colors

Change Colors in the next drop-down menu in the toolbar. Choose the color scheme that best suits your needs (these can be aesthetic and complement the colors and theme of your brand).

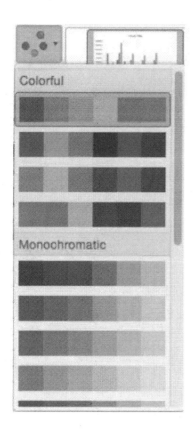

Adjusting chart colors

Change the Style

There are fourteen chart forms used for the charts (cluster column). The chart will be shown in Style 1 by default; however, you can adjust it. Click the arrow to the right of the picture bar to see further choices.

132

Adjusting chart styles

Switch Column/Row

To rotate the axes, click your toolbar's Switch Row/Column button. Notice that flipping axes for each chart often isn't helpful, for instance, if you have more than two variables.

Switching between Row and Column

Switching the column and row, in this case, flips the product and year (profit remains on the y-axis). The graph is now organized by product (rather than a year), and a color-coded legend corresponds to a year (not a product). To avoid doubt, go to the legend and change the Series to the actual years.

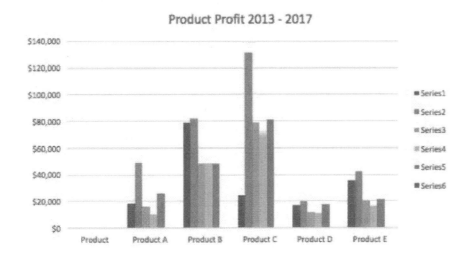

An example of switching Row/Column

Select the Data

To adjust the context of your files, click the Select Data button on the toolbar.

The select Data button

A window opens. Click the Ok button after typing in the cell set you want. This latest data set is reflected in the table automatically.

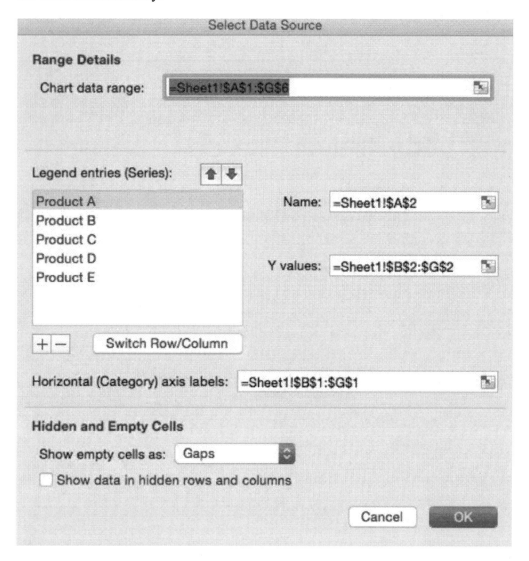

Choosing the data source

Change the Chart Type

Change a chart type from the drop-down menu.

How to change the chart type

You can adjust the chart category to Excel's nine chart types. But, again, it is essential to double-check that the data is suitable for the chart format you've chosen.

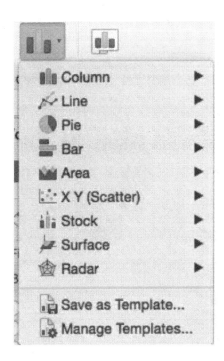

Chart Categories

You can save the chart as a template by pressing Save as Template.

You'll be presented with a dialogue box in which you can give your design a name. Excel can automatically generate a folder for the models to organize documents efficiently. To save your work, click the Save icon.

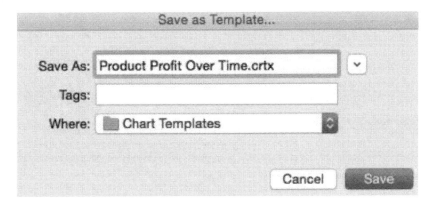

Saving as a template

Move a Chart

On the far right of your toolbar, click the Move Chart button.

Move
Chart

Moving a chart

You'll see a discussion box in which you can select where to put the chart. You can use this box to make a new layer (a New sheet) or use it as an entity in another sheet. To continue, press the blue OK key.

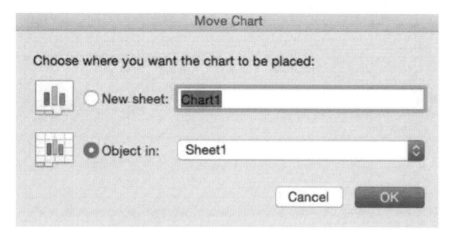

Selection position where to move your chart

Change the Formatting

You can adjust the colors, scale, design, fill, and orientation of all components and text in a chart and insert shapes using the Format tab. For example, to have a chart represent your company's brand or style, go to the Format tab and use an available shortcut (images, colors, etc.).

Changing the format of a chart

Select the chart feature you want to update from the drop-down menu on the top-left of your toolbar.

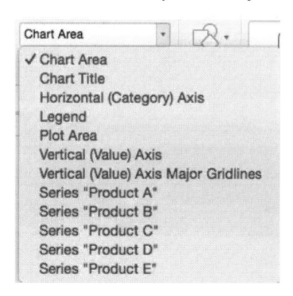

The chart features

Delete a Chart

Choose a chart and press the Delete button on the keyboard to delete it.

Printing Charts

Select the desired chart within your cookbook

Click on File, then select Print

Set your printer and the number of copies you need

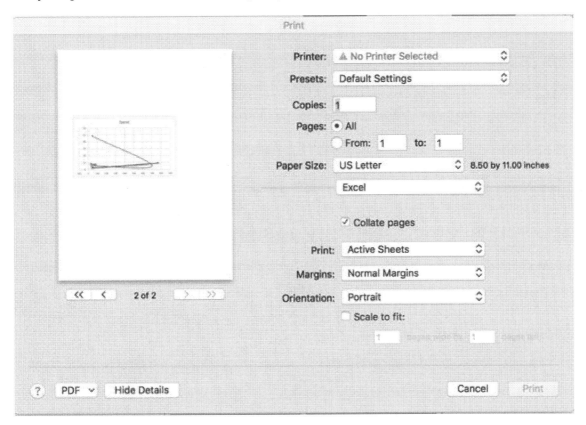

Selecting the print option

Click the Print Icon

Creating Charts in Excel

Charts are a wonderful method to communicate facts and information visually. The data that charts depict is their basis. The first and most significant step in producing a chart is selecting the appropriate data. You must first enter your data into Excel. Then, by moving your mouse across the cells containing the data you wish to utilize in your graph, you can highlight them. You may now choose your chart type to display your data after entering your data and selecting the cell range.

	A	B	C	D	E
1	Month	Bears	Dolphins	Whales	
2	Jan	8	150	80	
3	Feb	54	77	54	
4	Mar	93	32	100	
5	Apr	116	11	76	
6	May	137	6	93	
7	Jun	184	1	72	
8					

For example, suppose you have a spreadsheet with two data columns. The variable Year is in column A, while the variable Value is in column B. You wish to make a chart with the variable value on the vertical axis and the year on the horizontal axis.

After choosing your data for the chart, insert a chart into your spreadsheet using the instructions below:

1. Choose the information you want to use.

2. On the ribbon, select the Insert tab.

3. On the ribbon, select Insert Chart.

4. To see the previews, navigate through the Chart settings.

5. Please insert the desired chart by clicking on it. For example, in the figure below line chart is used.

6. A menu with several chart types appears when you click the line chart icon.

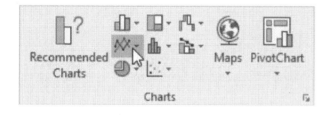

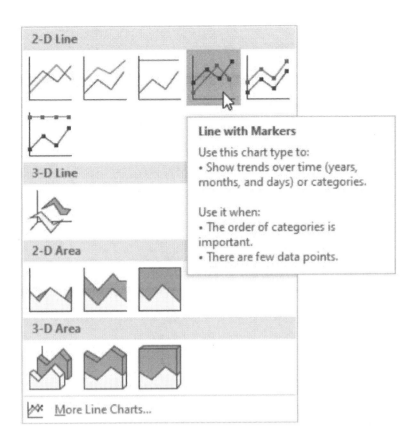

7. To create the chart, you must first tell Excel what data to use. Then, after selecting the chart canvas (by just clicking on it), go to the "Chart Design" tab and choose "Select Data" (see below). Alternatively, you can right-click the graph and select "Select Data."

8. The menu below shows how to pick data. You may pick the whole data region to be used at the top. You may choose which data to display on the left panel's vertical axis (y-axis) and which variable to display on the right panel's horizontal axis (x-axis).

9. Let's tell Excel what data to utilize for the vertical axis first. Then, as indicated below, click "Add."

10. A menu should now display identically to the one below. You may give the series a name and describe its content here. In addition, you may manually type the sequence described in the "Series name" field.

11. For the "Series Values," click the arrow up icon. Then, select all of the cells containing the values you want to display on the vertical axis.

12. To pick the series for the horizontal axis, go to the right panel and click "Edit." Then, select the data for the horizontal axis using the same technique as for the vertical axis and click OK.

13. To complete the "Select Data" operation, click "OK."

14. Your Chart will be inserted into your worksheet.

To make any chart, follow the procedures shown above. The technique for selecting data stays the same.

How to modify Excel Charts

Once the chart is in Excel, you may change its appearance and location in various ways. A few options are shown below:

- To add any labels (such as the title or axis), click Add Chart Element in the Chart Layouts group on the Design ribbon and choose the desired label.
- Use the Chart Tools Design ribbon to alter the chart type, data, or location.
- After selecting an element on the chart, you can choose the Format Selection icon in the Current Selection group from the Chart Tools Format ribbon. Next, you can adjust the text's shape, style, and color using the Formatting Task window.

How to Create a Process- Behavior Chart in Excel

The process-behavior chart, also known as a control chart, is frequently used to identify if a manufacturing or business process is statistically controlled. The processes for making a control chart in Excel are outlined below.

1. Arrange Data:

Of course, the first step is to enter the data you've gathered into the spreadsheet. Then, fill in the blanks with your data in rows, one for each sample. Each sample observation will be recorded in the sample's row as a separate cell. It would be perfect if you could additionally take advantage of headings to assist you in maintaining track of what's what.

2. Calculate Sample Statistics:

You will compute sample statistics for each control chart, including the average and range of the data plotted on the control chart. These statistics should be calculated using conventional Excel formulas on the same row as the relevant sample. The data's average is determined with the average function, while the range is derived with the maximum and minimum functions.

3. Calculate Center Line and Control Limits

The next step is to calculate the control chart's major components. The upper control limit (UCL) and lower control limit (LCL) are two control limits. To determine these limitations, you must first determine the Centerline. The average or media of your data is equal to the Center Line. Upper control limits are always set three standard deviations above the mean value, while lower control limits are set below.

Creating Process- Behavior Chart

Following are the steps to construct a control chart after you've selected all of the necessary data:

- Navigate to the Insert tab to create a Line Chart.

- Click on the Charts tab on the ribbon.

- Select the desired chart from the Insert Line chart selection list.

- Select the OK option.

- Your spreadsheet will add to the chart.

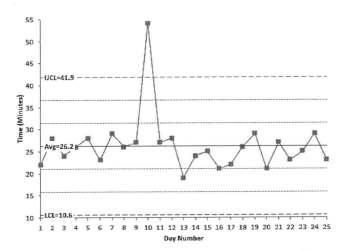

Chapter 11: Using Excel for Data Analysis

To conduct a successful data analysis in Excel, you need to know some fundamental things. First, you must understand the importance of data analysis within your company. Microsoft Excel assists us in overcoming this linguistic barrier and transforming raw statistics into ideas, patterns, and insights, for example.

Visualizing your data is essential when developing effective charts for your information. Unfortunately, only a few managers have the time to evaluate data in Excel manually. So instead, the findings are brought to life through the use of charts.

Process of carrying out data analysis

Navigating through a mountain of information might seem like a nightmare. When dealing with vast amounts of data simultaneously, studying and digesting the information might not be easy.

Remember, not all data is helpful or essential in some way. To make things worse, data in its raw form is often more confusing than informative.

First and foremost, before you can extract any form of actionable insight from your data, it must be collected, filtered, cleaned, visualized, analyzed, and then reported. The data analysis process is comprised of all of these components. Each time you undertake data analysis, the method may differ from the previous one. It is possible that unique hurdles and problems may occur, making it difficult to reach a decision. As a result, it is preferable to have dynamic solutions to deal with all of the unforeseen bumps on the road.

Excel's comprehensive range of features provides an excellent jump-start to the process. It is an easy tool to gather, organize, and organize data. Still, it can also be used to conduct sophisticated calculations and show the data using some basic charting capabilities, which is very useful. So, what is the best way to examine data in Excel? You may even be able to gain some fundamental insights from the information included in your

spreadsheet. So, you may run some basic analysis directly from your spreadsheets before charting or delving further into the statistics if you like.

Step 1: Specifying Data Requirements for a Project

To undertake efficient data analysis, you must first define the requirements for the data being analyzed. As part of this process, you must determine the structure and data types relevant to your investigation.

For marketing audiences, data needs may include their age, income, geography, and other demographic information. These criteria will influence the kind of information that must be gathered.

Step 2: Information Gathering

It is necessary to gather all the required data relating to these areas once you have established the variables and arranged them into categories. Your information must be comprehensive and correct to the greatest extent feasible.

Ultimately, it is your responsibility to guarantee that your data is accurately sourced and of high quality and accuracy. The information must still be filtered and cleaned before it can be used.

Step 3: Information and Communications Technology (ICT)

After collecting raw data, it is necessary to arrange it for additional analysis. First, you must organize the information into appropriate groups. Then, you will need to input the data into a spreadsheet or create a data model to organize the information properly. Organizing data in this manner makes it easy to filter and clean the inside information.

Step 4: Data Cleaning and Organization

Although the structured information may seem comprehensive and accurate, it is likely incomplete and includes mistakes or duplicate items. Therefore, it evaluates your gathered data and identifies and corrects any flaws or inconsistencies you may discover.

The collected data will determine how you should proceed with the cleaning procedure. For example, to check financial information, you may add up the totals and verify sure

they match the numbers in your records. This pre-review process is critical for determining the accuracy and dependability of the data items you have collected.

Step 5: Data Analysis and Interpretation

Once your data has gone through all the steps outlined above, it is ready for further investigation.

To execute the analytical process manually, you must physically examine each row and column of data and compare the totals while noting any patterns or other connections. If you have a large data collection, this may be exceedingly difficult and perhaps impossible to do successfully.

It is at this point that data visualization tools come in handy. By charting the data, you may visually examine the patterns, outliers, trends, and other data characteristics. This strategy may better comprehend your data in an extraordinarily short period.

Step 6: Communication

While the data analysis may seem to be the last phase, you must be able to discuss and convey your results to complete the process. In addition, you may be required to disclose your data insights to stakeholders, customers, team members, or other interested parties.

Everyone who will be reading your data must draw and comprehend the same conclusions as you did. However, it can convey the results effectively and understandably when data is complicated to explain without charts and other tools.

Why Data Analysis is Important to a Business

When you want to run a business, you need to analyze data in various ways. It will help you determine if your finances are unnecessary or if certain areas need improvement. You can also use data analysis to determine how much money you should spend on advertising, what products to produce, and whom to target. By understanding how your customers respond to your products, you will be able to determine how to spend your money wisely.

It will also help you to understand your customers better. Through data analysis, you can see which products are selling well and which ones do not. This will help you develop new products or services that appeal to your customers. Moreover, data analysis can also help you understand which areas you should focus on. For example, you can adjust your prices by understanding what your customers prefer and what they pay for. Furthermore, data analysis will help you improve your website targeting.

Data analysis is critical to a company's success. Without it, they cannot discover and utilize the knowledge they need to expand their business. It can also help businesses avoid filler activities, which may be detrimental to their bottom line. If you're wondering how to conduct data analysis in your company, consider using Andromeda's enterprise asset management software. These software packages allow companies to analyze data more effectively.

To get the most out of data analysis, businesses must develop a strategy to implement it. A solid strategy requires long-term planning and clear objectives. First, ask yourself: Why do you want to collect data? What are you hoping to accomplish with it? Next, determine the data sources and points and develop an action plan. Then, make sure you have a plan to make the best use of your new insights. Of course, you don't want to analyze data and hope for the best - you must make informed decisions!

Finally, data analysis can help you improve the quality of your customer experience. For example, storing data in a central location can easily predict what kind of customers will return to your website. Then, you can offer exclusive discounts to these customers. This will help your business improve in all areas. The quality of your customer experience will increase, and your customers will appreciate the extra effort. You'll be surprised at how much data your business will benefit from.

Major Functions in Data Analysis

A set of essential functions will significantly increase your capacity to interpret data, and you will wonder how you ever got by without them in the first place.

- **CONCATENATE**

Equation: =CONCATENATE(SELECT CELLS YOU WANT TO COMBINE)

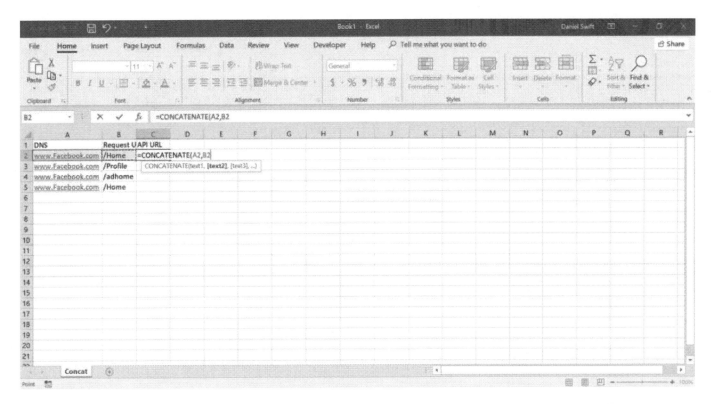

In this example: =CONCATENATE(A2,B2)

- **LEN**

Equation: =LEN(Mark Cell)

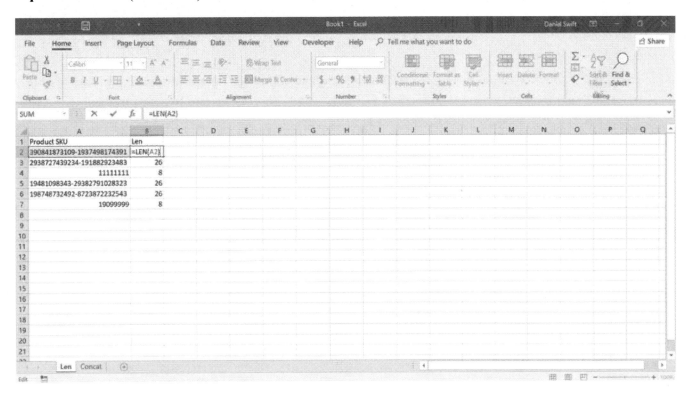

In the above figure: =LEN(A2)

- **COUNTA**

Equation: COUNTA(Mark Cell)

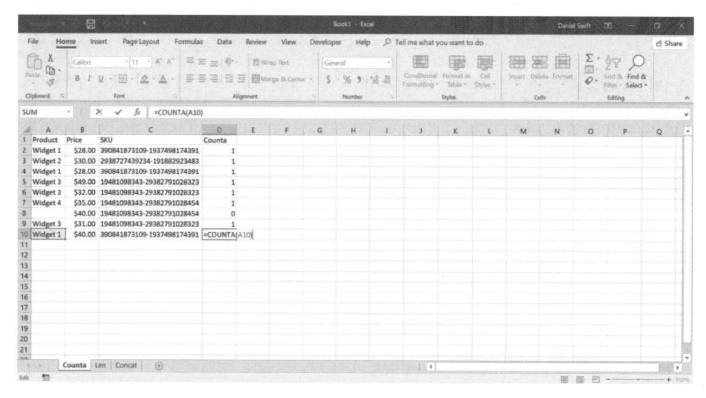

In the above figure: Count(A10)

- **Days or Network Days**

DAYS is precisely what the name describes it to be. This method calculates the number of calendar days that have elapsed between two dates using a calendar. A valuable tool for determining the lifespan of goods and contracts and deciding run rating income based on service duration is needed for data analysis.

NETWORKDAYS is a little more reliable and helpful than NETWORKDAYS. This formula calculates the number of "workdays" that have elapsed between two dates, with the option to take into account holidays. Even workaholics need a vacation from time to time! Using these two algorithms to compare periods is extremely beneficial in project management.

Equations: =DAYS (Mark CELL, Mark CELL)

=NETWORK DAYS (Mark CELL, Mark CELL....

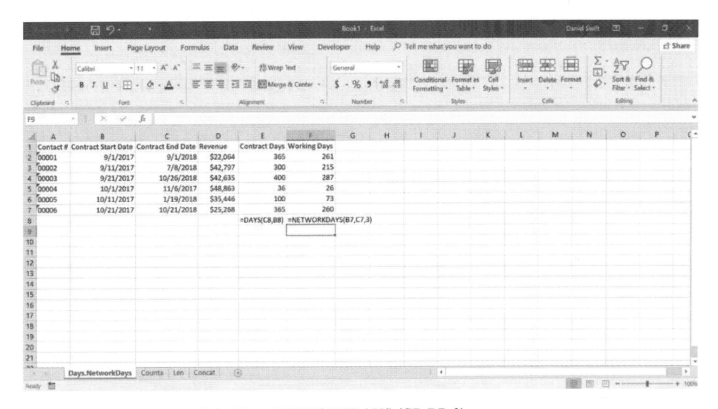

In the figure: =DAYS (B8, C8) OR   =NETWORKDAYS (C7, B7, 3)

- **SUMIFS**

Equation: =SUMIFS(sum range, criteria range 1, criteria 1, …)

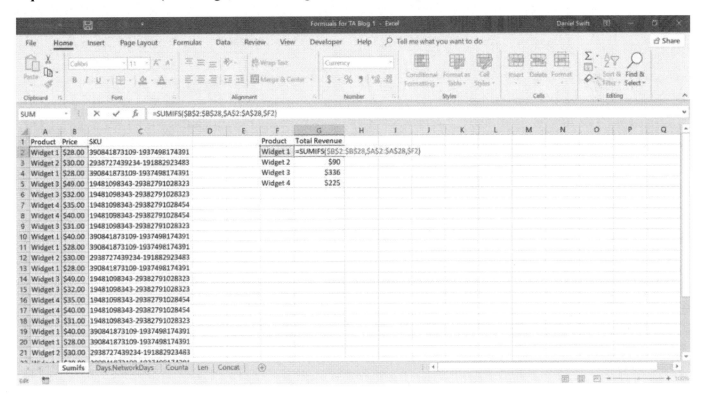

In figure: =SUMIFS(C2:C9,B2:B9,E3)

147

- **AverageIFS**

AVERAGEIFS works similarly to SUMIFS, enabling you to take an average based on one or more criteria.

Equation: =AVERAGEIF(SELECT CELL, CRITERIA)

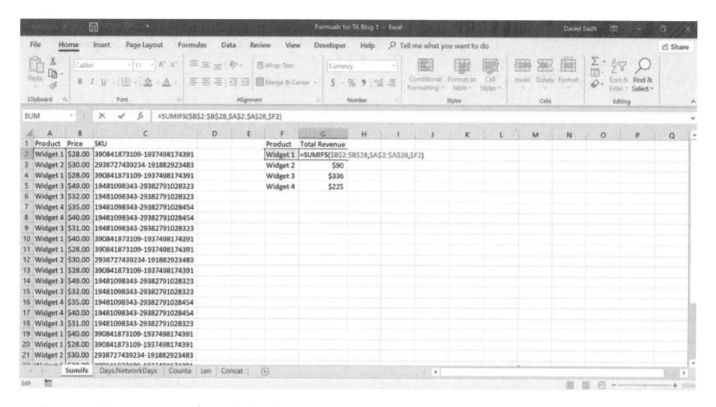

In the example: =AVERAGEIF($C:$C,$A:$A,$F2)

- **VLOOKUP**

VLOOKUP is one of the globally widely used and well-known data analysis functions. If you're an Excel user, you'll almost certainly need to "marry" data together at some time in your career. For example, accounts receivable may be aware of the cost of each product, but the shipping department may only offer the number of units that have been dispatched. That is the ideal application for the VLOOKUP function.

Using reference data (A2) in conjunction with the price table, Excel can search for matching criteria in the first column and return an adjacent value, as seen in the figure below.

Equation: =VLOOKUP (LOOKUP VALUE, TABLE ARRAY, COL INDEX NUM, [RANGE LOOKUP])

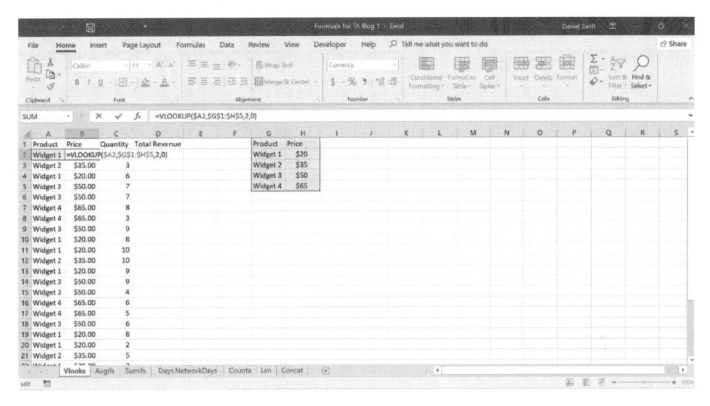

In the example: =VLOOKUP($A2,$G$1:$H$5,2,0)

- **FIND/SEARCH**

For finding particular text inside a data collection, the =FIND/=SEARCH methods are quite effective. Both are included because =FIND will return case-sensitive results, i.e.,

If you use FIND to query for "Big," you will only get results that are Big=true. However, a =SEARCH for "Big" will return results for both Big and big, broadening the scope of the query. Searching for anomalies or unique IDs is a particularly beneficial use of this technique.

Equation:=FIND(TEXT,WITHIN_TEXT,[START_NUMBER])
=SEARCH(TEXT,WITHIN_TEXT,[START_NUMBER])

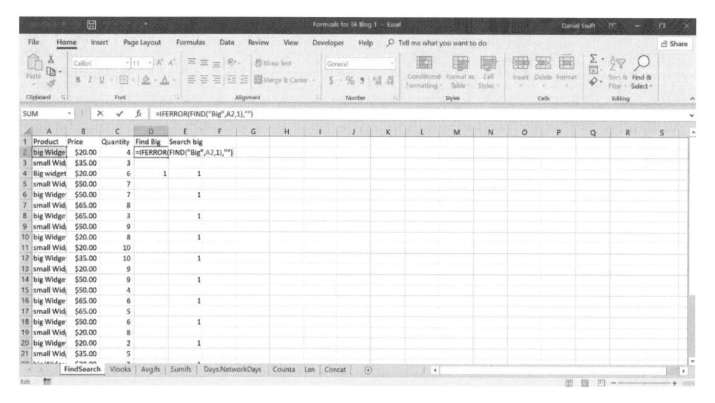

In the example: =(FIND("Big", A2,1)""

Chapter 12: Security in a Spreadsheet and Workbook

Does your bank send your statement of account to your email address every month? If your bank does that, you will discover you don't just open that file without typing any security password to access it in some cases. It can be a few digits from your account number.

Security is essential in most things we do in life. You lock your doors properly before you sleep every night because of security. You use a password, pattern, or PIN to lock your smartphone because of Security. Security is essential for our safety.

Concerning that, Microsoft built their Excel with a good security feature so that someone doesn't just view what is contained in the file without a password. For example, suppose you are sending your workers' earnings to some top officers in your company. In that case, there may be a need to lock it with a password because that is sensitive information that everybody does not need to access. On sending the file to the top officers, you share the password they need to insert before they can view the content. Any other person without a password cannot view the data contained in the file.

How to Lock a Worksheet with a Password

Whether worksheet or spreadsheet, we discuss the same area of interest. To protect a spreadsheet, click the spreadsheet name example, sheet1, sheet2, sheet3 (but if there's only one sheet in that workbook, there is no need to click the spreadsheet name).

The next step you need to take is to click the Review tab of Excel. Click Protect Sheet command. This action will open the sheet protection dialogue box, which I have in the photo below.

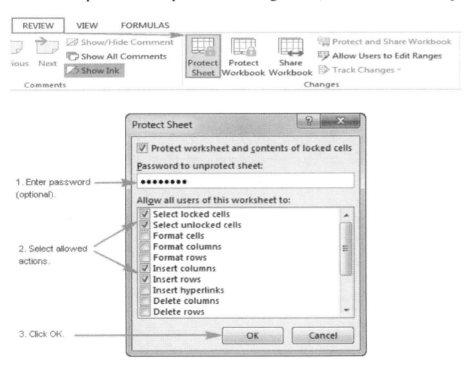

151

The sheet protection dialogue box

In the space for Password to unprotect the sheet, type the password you want to use to lock the worksheet. Click the Ok button. Excel will request you type the password you previously typed for the sheet protection. Just enter the same password and click the OK button again. Once Excel confirms that the password you re-entered is correct, the sheet becomes locked. That is all on how you can protect a worksheet.

How to Secure Workbook with Password

In the same way, you locked a worksheet with a password. You can still secure your workbook with a password. Know that workbook has more than one spreadsheet inside of it. I explained this in chapter 1 under terminology used in Excel.

To protect a workbook with a password, take these steps:

Click the Review tab of your Excel. As you click the tab, you will see some commands. Just click the Protect Workbook command. This action will open a dialogue box. In the space for you to type the password you want to use to lock the workbook, just type the password you can remember. Click the OK button at the bottom part of the dialogue box. Excel will demand you repeat the password. Type the same password and click the OK button. By doing that, the entire workbook becomes protected with the password.

Chapter 13: Errors in Microsoft Excel

10 Excel Error Messages.

Common Errors in Excel

Let's get jiggy.

Error

Understand the problem: This error code indicates that either the column width of a cell is too narrow for the cell's contents or you entered a date earlier than 01.01.1900. In some versions of Excel, the format "date" allows you to work only up to the year 1900.

How to resolve the issue: If the column width is too narrow, just drag it wider with the mouse or, as described at the beginning of the book, double-click in the space between two columns (alternatively, you can also reduce the font size). If you wish to enter a date before 1900, you will be forced to work without the "date" format (use the format "number").

Error #NUM!

Understand the problem: This error happens when you use a number in a calculation that is either too large or too tiny for Excel (but only for extremely large or extremely small integers) or if the computation is mathematically incorrect or, at the very least unsolvable in Excel (for example, square root of a negative number). However, dividing by "0," a different error code is displayed.

How to resolve the problem: Rectify it if you made a simple typing error. Suppose you genuinely need to work with extremely large or small numbers or complex numbers (for example, to solve the square root of a negative number). In that case, you should consider using another calculation application (e.g., Matlab from Mathworks).

Error #VALUE!

Understand the problem: This error will be displayed if you attempt calculations by mistakenly referencing cells with various or incorrect cell formats. Additionally, likely, the calculation is not done at all. Addition of a "number" formatted cell to a "text" formatted cell (but can still contain a number; the formatting is essential). You receive the formula as text in the cell, for example, "=A1+B2".

How to Solve the problem: When calculating numbers, utilize identical formattings, such as "number" or the format "standard" (which does not define a specific format).

Error #NA

Understand the problem: For instance, if you apply the VLOOKUP, HLOOKUP, or LOOKUP functions in your spreadsheet, an error may occur. It implies that a particular value could not be located.

How to Solve the problem: Include the value you're looking for in the range you're searching for or use another value as a reference. Usually, this is a simple spelling error.

Error #NULL!

Understand the problem: This error frequently occurs when a formula is misused. Often, a range is not properly addressed here and hence is not recognized by Excel. For instance, =SUM (A1:A10 B1:B10). This specification would result in the #NULL! Error because the range specification lacks a separator element denoted by a ";" The correct syntax is =SUM (A1:A10; B1:B10).

How to solve the problem: Check the cells in the formula range with missing signs and add them. It is often only a ";" or brackets that are missing.

Error #NAME?

Understand the problem: When text is used in formulas without quotation marks, this error code is returned: "Text." This can also occur if a function contains a mistake, for example, =Sun (A1:A10).

Solving the problem: Quote the text with double quotation marks and check for typos.

Error #DIV/0!

Understand the problem: This is a mathematical error when dividing a number by "0".

How to Solve the problem: Seriously, why would you want to divide anything by zero!?

Error #REF!

Understand the problem: Excel displays this error when you reference or Find something that does not exist in the spreadsheet. For example, this may result from referencing a cell from another spreadsheet in a formula or a cell you have moved or deleted.

How to Solve the problem: Double-Check

Circular Reference

Understand the problem: A pop-up window warning about a "circular reference" appears. Cyclical reference refers to the fact that a cell refers to itself, resulting in a circular process. This may arise, for example, if a cell in which you wish to display the result of a calculation appears within the calculation itself, e.g., =TOTAL(A1:A10). You want to show the result in cell A1.

How to solve the problem: You must select another cell to display the result or check whether cells refer to themselves.

Number becomes Date

Understand the problem: Sometimes, Excel can stupidly convert a number you input to a date.

How to solve the problem: Check the cell formatting. Change it to the "standard" or "number" format. When this happens, it means Excel is not "stupid" you (or a prankster) have formatted the cell to show "date," and so whatever you input will be displayed as a date.

Chapter 14: Macros In MS Excel

A macro in Excel is nothing more than a set of instructions that are repeated over and over. Following the creation of a macro, Excel will step-by-step carry out the instructions on whatever data you supply.

Consider the following scenario: we write a macro in Excel that instructs the program to take a number, add two, multiply by five, and then return the number's modulus.

- Now, anytime we tell Excel to execute the macro, we don't have to worry about going through each step manually; Excel will take care of everything for us.
- A macro can be used to record almost any type of information. As a result, it's possible to perform numerical computations, text operations, formatting, and cell movement in any way you can.
- When you continuously repeat the same steps, macros can save you a substantial amount of time. While this may not seem like much initially, it can add up over time.
- Suppose you're formatting raw data, filtering and sorting data, or simply repeating a sequence of functions and actions on your sheets. In that case, you're on the right track.
- Also useful for sharing, macros are stored in Excel spreadsheets, so you don't have to send any additional files to your colleagues because they are contained within the spreadsheet. Instead, simply construct a macro, hand over the spreadsheet to them, and let them get to work on the project.
- If you routinely work with spreadsheets, there is a good chance that you may save a significant amount of time by utilizing macros.

How to create a macro in Microsoft Excel

- Before you can utilize Excel macros to automate your chores, you must first "record" a macro in Excel.
- Excel should take steps when the macro is executed can be specified by recording the macro.
- Additionally, whereas Visual Basic for Applications (VBA) can be used to construct a macro, Excel allows you to record an Excel macro using standard commands rather than Visual Basic for Applications (VBA).

Consider the following straightforward example.

	A	B	C	D	E	F	G
1							
2							
3							
4	East	Technical Support	800	650	700	2150	
5	East	Telephone	900	850	850	2600	
6	East	Copying	4850	3200	1155	9205	
7	East	Overhead	1250	1250	1250	3750	
8	East	Software	2025	2200	1650	5875	
9	East	Maintenance	1350	1500	1700	4550	
10	East	Supplies	3300	3500	3700	10500	
11	East	Telemarketing	3825	3725	3750	11300	
12	East	Contractors	8900	10315	5250	24465	
13	East	Consultants	6250	6000	6500	18750	
14	East	Rent	8000	8000	8000	24000	
15	East	Miscellaneous	11500	12500	12500	36500	
16	East	Advertising	12250	12250	12750	37250	
17	East	Clerical Support	25000	24000	26390	75390	
18							

- Customize the ribbon by going to File > Options and selecting Customize Ribbon from the sidebar. Then, in the Main Tabs, make sure the Developer checkbox is selected:

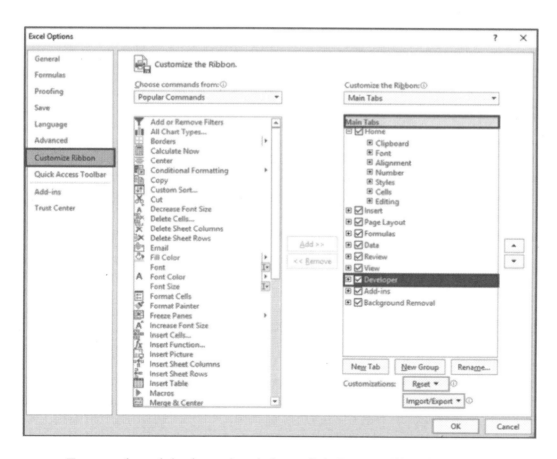

- To open that tab in the main window, click OK. You'll notice a Record Macro button.

- Simply click that button to begin recording a macro.

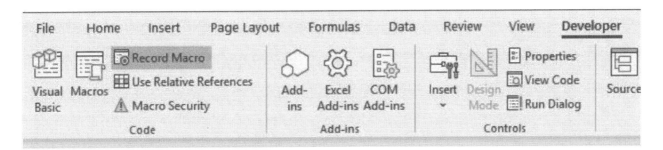

- If you want to name your macro (we named ours "Macro1") and specify a shortcut key, you'll be prompted for that information.
- It is important to remember that there is already a variety of Ctrl-based shortcuts available; avoid overwriting the ones that you use frequently.

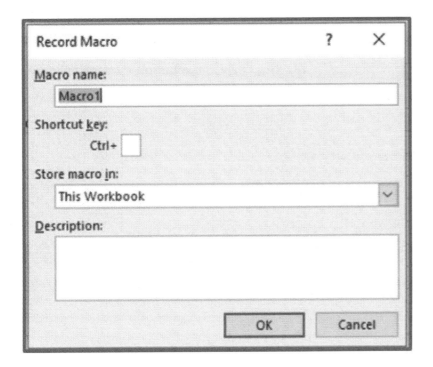

- You also have three options for storing the macro: in the current workbook, a new workbook, or one of your macro workbooks.
- This workbook (personal.xlsb) contains macros that can be executed on any workbook that you can access in Excel.
- You can use it to store all of your Excel macros in a centralized location for easy access.
- If you're building a macro that will only be used in this spreadsheet, save it there. If, on the other hand, you believe you may need to reuse the macro in another worksheet, you should keep it in your macro workbook for ease of access.
- Once you click OK, Excel will keep track of everything you do.

The following are the steps we will take:

Enable filtering

Sort column B from largest to smallest

Copy cell B2

Paste in cell E2

Copy cell A2

Paste in cell E3

Make cells E2 and E3 bold

- To record a macro, simply click Record Macro, follow the on-screen instructions, and then click Stop Recording.
- Once you start recording, the Record Macro button is replaced by the Stop Recording button, which you can use to end the recording.
- Each of those activities is standard; for example, clicking the Filter button, sorting using the dropdown filter arrow, and copying the cell with the Ctrl + C keyboard shortcut.
- A macro can be created using just this information! Press the record button, conduct some actions, and then press the stop button.

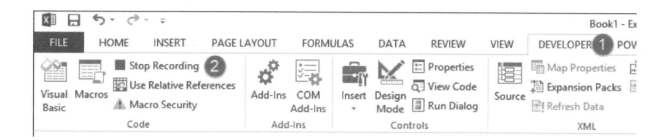

How to run a macro in Excel

After saving your macro, you can execute it in various ways.

- To get started, you can launch it immediately from the Ribbon menu. A Macros button can be found on the application's View and the Developer tabs. To see your macros, click on the corresponding icon.
- You can select and execute any macro you've already saved from the resulting window. Then, choose it and press the Run button.
- Excel will retrace the steps you took throughout the record-keeping session.
- To ensure it was successful, unbold and delete cells E2 and E3 in the sample worksheet and then arrange the names alphabetically in the new worksheet.

- When you run the macro, you should get the same result as when you ran it before.
- The shortcut key that you used to save your macro can also be used to run it. For example, ctrl + the key combination you entered in the save box.
- Adding a shortcut key afterward is as simple as navigating to View Macros, selecting the macro, and selecting Options. Creating a new shortcut key will be an option when you log in.

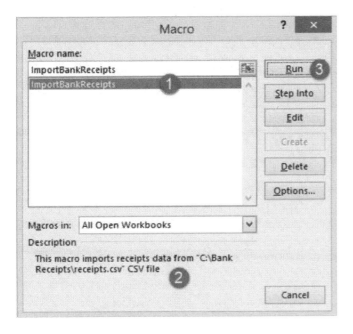

- To add a shortcut key later, navigate to View Macros, select the macro, and then click Options in the shortcut key field. Then, create a new shortcut key available to you after the installation is complete.

A button on the spreadsheet that will execute the macro can be created if you regularly run a complex macro or share your spreadsheet with others.

This is how you do it.

- To begin, create a form; in this case, a rectangle with rounded corners will suffice.

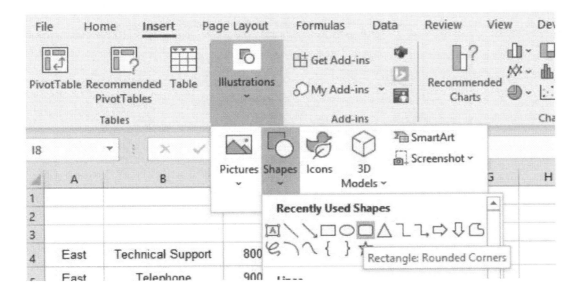

- In the Shape Editor, you can add text to the shape that describes what it does by right-clicking and selecting Edit Text.

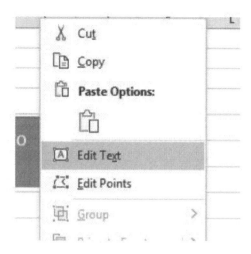

- Now, right-click the shape and choose Assign Macro from the context menu.

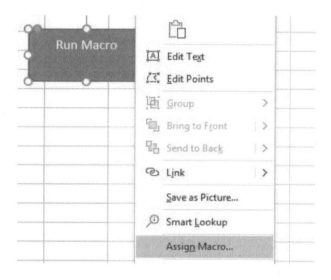

- After selecting the corresponding macro from the subsequent window, click OK to confirm your selection.
- After that, every time you click on that shape, Excel will run the macro you previously recorded!

The final option is to run macros directly from the Quick Access Toolbar.

- You must, however, first add the View Macros button to the Quick Access Toolbar before you can use it.
- Select File > Options from the menu bar, and then Quick Access Toolbar from the left-hand pane:
- To add it to the Quick Access Toolbar, scroll to the bottom of the list and select View Macros, followed by the Add >> button.
- Click on the OK button.
- Simply click the macros button at the top of the Excel window to start a macro right away:

Zone	Category	Jan.	Feb	Mar	Total
East	Technical Support	800	650	700	2150
East	Telephone	900	850	850	2600
East	Copying	4850	3200	1155	9205
East	Overhead	1250	1250	1250	3750
East	Software	2025	2200	1650	5875
East	Maintenance	1350	1500	1700	4550
East	Supplies	3300	3500	3700	10500
East	Telemarketing	3825	3725	3750	11300
East	Contractors	8900	10315	5250	24465
East	Consultants	6250	6000	6500	18750
East	Rent	8000	8000	8000	24000
East	Miscellaneous	11500	12500	12500	36500
East	Advertising	12250	12250	12750	37250
East	Clerical Support	25000	24000	26390	75390

Run Macro

Chapter 15: Excel and Everyday Life

Microsoft Excel stores and analyzes data in a numerical format in spreadsheet software. A spreadsheet is a collection of rows and columns that form a table. Unlike numbers, letters of the alphabet are allocated to columns, while numbers are assigned to rows. Rows and columns come together at a position known as a cell, and the cell address is a letter representing a row in the table of contents. In addition, Microsoft Excel may include graphical tools, computations, pivot tables, and basic visual programs, a programming language for creating macros (also known as macro programming). In addition, it has a battery of functions that provide solutions to technical, financial, and statistical questions. Furthermore, Excel can display data in line graphs, charts, and histograms, with only a limited ability to display three-dimensional visual data.

Keeping Costs Under Control

Individuals commonly utilize it to complete tasks since it provides several advantages. Managing expenses is made easier with the help of Microsoft Excel. Suppose a teacher receives a monthly income of around 60,000 dollars. He will need to record his costs and utilize Microsoft Excel to determine the precise amount he will spend each month. These are accomplished by entering monthly pay and spending

information into Excel tables, allowing you to track and manage costs appropriately. Managing expenditures is one of the most effective applications of Microsoft Excel in everyday life.

Consolidates Data into a Single Place

The incredible feature of Microsoft Excel is the ability to integrate a large number of data into a single spot. It has the benefit of preventing data from being lost accidentally. The information is maintained in a single place. As a result, you will save time by not searching for files. You must organize and classify data to save time when retrieving information from a file when needed.

Access to Information Through The Internet

Microsoft Excel can be accessed online from any location, meaning you may access it from any device, location, or time. It offers handy working facilities, which means that you may use your mobile phone to do your tasks even if you do not have access to a personal computer. Finally, since it offers a high degree of adaptability, it allows individuals to utilize it easily without getting concerned about their location or device.

It Makes Data Display More Illuminating

Using Microsoft Excel facilitates the display of data in a more illuminating manner. It benefits from making data bars more effective, identifying certain files by highlighting them, and presenting data visually appealingly. For example, if you have data in Excel and need to draw attention to a certain section of it, you will utilize several aspects of MS Excel's data presentation to do this. In addition, spreadsheets may be designed to be more visually attractive to the data stored in them.

Security

Because the primary use of Microsoft Excel is to provide security, consumers can keep their information secure. The stored files in this program may be protected using a personal password code, which prevents them from being accessed or destroyed by others. These may be entered into the excel spreadsheet or created using simple visual programming. Another advantage of using Excel is that it keeps important data structured and requires less time to access it than other data storage methods. The usage of Microsoft Excel allows for the quick resolution of problems.

Formulate Your Thoughts in Mathematical Terms

The mathematical formulae that may be discovered in Microsoft Excel make work more convenient. Complex arithmetic problems may be addressed straightforwardly without requiring additional human effort. The program has several formulae that you may use to solve problems, such as determining the average and total simultaneously on large amounts of data. As a result, Excel is the most effective tool for obtaining answers and using the fundamental functions of mathematics that may be found in tables containing enormous amounts of data.

Recovering Information from Spreadsheets and Databases

If data is lost, Microsoft Excel makes it possible to retrieve it without causing any hardship. If your critical data is lost or destroyed, and the data is stored in Excel, you no longer need to be concerned since the new version of Excel has a format for recovering lost or damaged data. Additionally, it offers features such as spreadsheets that make work easier and the XML format, which reduces the size of spreadsheets to make files more compact while working with large files.

Make Your Job More Convenient

Microsoft Excel includes several tools that simplify the process and take a short time. The offered tool may filter, sort, and search for data to make the job more convenient for you. You may also combine the tools with pivot tables and tables to expedite the completion of your task. It allows numerous items from big data sets to be examined with minimal effort, and it aids in discovering answers to questions and issues.

There has been an improvement in time management.

You'll have to deal with many tasks daily if you want to be a successful business owner and manager or even just an employee in a large firm. You will need to be productive and efficient in your operations to be successful as a result. Excel's multiple features come in handy in this situation.

If you are acquainted with Excel's often-used shortcuts, you may increase your productivity while improving your time management abilities. Become familiar with all of Excel's commonly used shortcuts. Additionally, macros and other formulas may be used to automate your tasks on a computer. When you take advantage of the subtle pushes that Excel gives, you can free up a significant amount of time to focus on more challenging tasks. In contrast, Excel takes care of most of the routine, repetitive, formula-based work for you.

Take a thorough examination of the facts

When dealing with a large amount of data, it can get confusing due to the process. Consequently, you will have difficulties extracting major patterns and resources from the data you have at your disposal if you prefer to analyze data quantitatively. You will thus be unable to make accurate predictions from the data you have at your disposal.

Microsoft Excel may be useful in this situation. The program offers you features such as conditional formatting, which enables you to highlight rows that satisfy particular criteria. In addition, having a visual representation of all the data will free up your time. You will no longer be limited to focusing on individual data points but will be able to consider a complete picture and make predictions that are more likely to be true.

Excel also allows you to create several graphical representations, such as pie charts, graphs, histograms, and more, to make data presentation simpler to grasp and to make it more visually appealing. As a result, everyone in your organization, group, or project will be on the same page regarding their interpretation of the data being given as a result of this collaboration.

Calculations that are both quicker and more accurate

With the use of Excel formulas, you can do calculations more rapidly and automatically than you would otherwise be able to do by hand. If you are knowledgeable in Excel, you will not need to do complicated number calculations manually, which is both time-consuming and prone to human error in most cases. You will also be able to do even the most complex calculations and operations in a matter of clicks, without wasting any time and with no sacrifice to even the slightest degree of accuracy, as a result of your mastery of advanced Excel concepts and information.

Improvements in one's ability to analyze information

In particular, regarding analytics and calculations, Microsoft Excel offers pupils a wealth of creative alternatives. Comprehending economics is an essential aspect of operating a successful business. An absence of analytical ability among individuals in charge of evaluating financial accounts and other critical indicators has caused many organizations to suffer. Students benefit from the use of Excel since it provides them with the knowledge and talents they need to be successful in their academic activities as well as their future professional

endeavors. As a result of its use in the administration, analysis, and execution of financial calculations in business and daily life, Excel may aid in the development of solid analytical talents.

Suppose you can show expertise in financial management and use Excel to do analytics even before you begin working for a firm. In that case, you will be a valuable asset to the organization where you are employed. It is also probable that the company where you will be employed already uses Excel or a similar piece of software to which you will be accustomed. As a result of your practical experience, you'll be well-prepared to build a name for yourself in the professional world.

Techniques and principles for data visualization

While Excel can do calculations and supply formulas, it also has a large selection of data visualization tools, as previously mentioned. In particular, data visualization is a precious talent when working with teams of people with various specialties. Not everyone in the firm can make sense of raw data provided in numbers, percentages, and statistical data. According to research, the vast majority of people prefer information to be presented in a visually attractive and easily consumable manner. When faced with a circumstance like this, multiple Excel visualization choices might be useful.

Using pie charts, bar charts, histograms, and other visual representations of data, you can show all of your data, outcomes, and future trends in a visually attractive style that will engage your audience. As a result, you'll be able to ensure that everyone in your organization — from marketing teams to sales teams, from engineers to senior management — is on the same page regarding all of the data, predictions, and decisions being made in your firm.

Moreover, more complex tools enable more accurate and higher-level data visualization. However, although students must be acquainted with Excel visualization techniques, it is even more crucial to have a good head start in their professions after graduation. For example, in the case of students pursuing a Bachelor of Business Administration or a Master of Business Administration degree, they have studied how to develop demand and supply curves, how to forecast the future based on data, how to compute net profit and profit margin, and how to forecast the future based on data. All of this may be easily reproduced in Excel to help students get a deeper and more comprehensive understanding of the content.

Chapter 16: Excel in Business Workspace and Marketplace

What are the uses of Microsoft Excel in the workplace? Or in the marketplace? If we list some of the ways that business uses MS Excel, it's quite long. But we've broken it down to just a few.

MS Excel is used for various tasks, including storing information, analyzing and sorting data, and reporting. Spreadsheets are incredibly popular in the corporate world because they are highly visual and relatively simple.

Business analysis, human resource management, performance reporting, and operations management are just a few of the many applications for Microsoft Excel that are often found in businesses. For example, we can confidently say that (using MS Excel) because we analyzed employment data.

1. Business Analysis

Business analysis is the most popular usage of MS Excel at work.

Business analysis is fundamentally data-driven decision-making. For example, businesses naturally collect data on product sales, website traffic, supply costs, insurance claims, etc.

Company analysis is the practice of making data relevant to business owners. You might, for example, run a profitability report on a weekday. If the company consistently loses money on Sundays, management may use that data to make decisions (such as closing on Sundays).

2. People Management

One of the most actual applications of Excel in the company is managing people.

Employees, clients, sponsors, or training participants may all be organized in MS Excel.

Personal data may be saved and accessed effectively with Excel. For example, a spreadsheet row or column may include an individual's name, email address, employee start date, purchases, subscription status, and last contact.

3. Office Administration

Office administrators utilize Microsoft Excel to input and store critical administrative data. For example, it is possible to utilize the same data for accounting and financial reporting.

Excel is also essential in office administration for invoicing, bill payment, and contacting suppliers and customers. So it's a multi-purpose office management tool.

4. Project Management

An Excel Workbook can be an excellent alternative to PM software.

Projects are commercial activities with a budget and a timeline. Project plans may be entered into a workbook to monitor progress and keep the project on track.

Using Excel allows you to simply share the project workbook with others, particularly those unfamiliar with or unable to use proprietary PM software.

5. Managing Problems

Excel is an excellent program manager. It may be tailored to a particular program's needs. It's also easy to switch managers since MS Excel is commonly used.

Like a project, a program requires user input and may be ongoing. Manage resources, monitor progress, and retain participant information using MS Excel.

6. Contract Administration

Contract administrators like to utilize Microsoft Excel since it is a simple tool for documenting contract data, such as dates, milestones, deliverables, and payment amounts.

There are many different contract management templates available, and each may be customized to meet the specific contract type or stage of the contract lifecycle being used.

7. Account Management

Account managers must be proficient in MS Excel since they receive and maintain client records.

An account manager's role is to cultivate current customer connections. To increase client loyalty and repeat purchases. It's a marketing position and a popular MBA profession.

Excel is widely used in account administration because it allows easy file sharing and maintenance.

Learning Excel is very tricky and complicated, I know. But it will be worth the number of new jobs you can apply to.

Not so sure if you want to pay money for Excel classes quite yet? You may change your mind when you see this list of careers that require it.

- Administrative Assistants

- Accountants

- Cost Estimator

- Project Manager

- Financial Analyst

- Business Analyst

- Data Analyst

- Information Clerk

These are some of the careers you might want to explore using your Excel skills.

Excel is here to stay, and organizations will continue to rely on it as their main tool for various tasks and applications, ranging from information technology initiatives to workplace picnics.

A solid understanding of Excel is essential for most office-based workers today, and improving one's Excel abilities may open the door to advancement and leadership chances in the workplace. Excel is a strong tool, but it cannot do all the tasks independently. It takes a competent computer user to use everything that Excel has to offer to provide the finest outcomes possible for their company's needs.

You need to include your knowledge of Excel in your Resume! Make it interesting that you know it, and boom! You will be found as a person who will do their Excel work for them.

Conclusion

Microsoft Excel can be a powerful productivity tool if used properly. The time you spend learning how to use it will be well worth the effort when you've saved reports and documents in your version of Excel.

This book has given you some basic knowledge about Microsoft Excel and increased your skills so you can become familiar with the ins and outs of this application. Go ahead and practice more.

Joseph Thompson

Made in the USA
Las Vegas, NV
18 March 2023

69302032R00094